Official Rules of Softball

TRIUMPH

BOOKS

CHICAGO

Typographer: Sue Knopf

Front cover photo courtesy of the Amateur Softball Association

This book is available in quantity at special discounts for your
group or organization.

For further information, contact:

Triumph Books
644 South Clark Street
Chicago, IL 60605
Tel. (312) 939-3330
Fax (312) 663-3557

PRINTED IN CANADA

User's Guide

This new edition of the Official Rules of Softball as approved by
the Amateur Softball Association contains all the current rules
governing the playing of the game.

The book is divided into two main sections: the Rules of the Game
and Points of Emphasis. The Rules include all official definitions
and measurements, pitching regulations for fast pitch, modified
pitch, slow pitch, and 16-inch slow pitch, descriptions of the positions, and rules for umpires and protests. The Points of Emphasis
includes information on appeals and special playing situations. A
third section is an index that cross-references the Rules and the
Points of Emphasis. The appendices cover diagrams of the playing
field, modifications of the rules for the NAIA, the NCAA, and the
NJCAA. There is a detailed Table of Contents to assist you in
finding all the rules and information within.

Contents

PART 1
THE OFFICIAL PLAYING RULES

RULE 5
THE GAME

RULE 6
PITCHING REGULATIONS (Fast Pitch)

RULE 6
PITCHING REGULATIONS (MODIFIED PITCH)

RULE 6
PITCHING REGULATIONS (SLOW PITCH)

RULE 6
PITCHING REGULATIONS (16 INCH SLOW PITCH)

RULE 7
BATTING

RULE 8
BATTER-RUNNER AND RUNNER

RULE 9
PROTESTS

RULE 10
UMPIRES

RULE 11
SCORING

PART 2
POINTS OF EMPHASIS

Softball
Official Rules

Part One
THE OFFICIAL
PLAYING RULES

Wherever "he" or "him" or their related pronouns may appear in this rule book either as words or as parts of words, they have been used for literary purposes and are meant in their generic sense (i.e., to include all humankind, or both male and female sexes).

The words "Junior Olympic" or the initials "JO" refer to youth softball.

New rules and/or changes are identified by ruled boxes.

Read the "Points of Emphasis" at the end of the rules to clarify various selected rules.

RULE 1 - DEFINITIONS

ALTERED BAT. A bat is considered altered when the physical structure of a legal softball bat has been changed. Replacing the handle of a metal bat with a wooden or other type handle, inserting material inside the bat, applying excessive tape (more than two layers) to the bat grip or painting a bat at the top or bottom for other than identification purposes are examples of altering a bat. Replacing the grip with another legal grip is not considered altering the bat. A "flare" or "cone" grip attached to the bat is considered an altered bat.

APPEAL PLAY. An appeal play is a play on which an umpire may not make a decision until requested by a manager, coach or player. The appeal must be made before the next legal or illegal pitch or before the pitcher and all infielders have clearly vacated their normal fielding positions and have left fair territory on their way to the bench or dugout area. On the last play of the game, an appeal can be made until the umpires leave the field of play.

BASE ON BALLS. A base on balls permits a batter to gain first base without liability to be put out and is awarded to a batter by the umpire when four pitches are judged to be balls. (Slow Pitch Only) If the pitcher desires to walk a batter intentionally, he may do so by notifying the plate umpire who shall award the batter first base.

BASE PATH. A base path is an imaginary line three feet (0.91m) on either side of a direct line between the bases.

BATTED BALL. A batted ball is any ball that hits the bat or is hit by the bat and lands either in fair or foul territory. No intent to hit the ball is necessary.

BATTER'S BOX. The batter's box is the area to which the batter is restricted. The lines are considered as being within the batter's box. Prior to the pitch, he may touch the lines, but no part of his foot may be outside the lines.

BATTER-RUNNER. A batter-runner is a player who has finished his turn at bat but has not yet been put out or touched first base.

BATTING ORDER. The batting order is the official listing of offensive players by first name, defensive position and uniform number in the order in which members of that team must come to bat.

BLOCKED BALL. A blocked ball is a batted or thrown ball that is touched, stopped or handled by a person not engaged in the game, or which touches any object that is not part of the official equipment or official playing area.

BLOOD RULE. Refers to a player, coach or umpire who is bleeding or who has blood on his uniform and treatment is required.

BUNT. A bunt is a legally tapped ball not swung at, but intentionally met with the bat and tapped slowly within the infield.

CATCH. A catch is a legally caught ball which occurs when the fielder catches a batted, pitched or thrown ball with his hand(s) or glove. In establishing a valid catch, the fielder shall hold the ball long enough to prove he has complete control of it or that his release of the ball is voluntary and intentional. If a player drops the ball after reaching into his glove to remove it or while in the act of throwing, it is a valid catch. If the ball is merely held in the fielder's arm(s) or prevented from dropping to the ground by some part of the fielder's body, equipment or

clothing, the catch is not completed until the ball is in
the grasp of the fielder's hand(s) or glove. It is not a catch
if a fielder, immediately after he contacts the ball, collides
with another player, umpire or a fence, or falls to the
ground and drops the ball as a result of the collision or
falling to the ground. A ball which strikes anything other
than a defensive player while it is in flight, is ruled the
same as if it struck the ground. An illegally caught ball
occurs when a fielder catches a batted or thrown ball
with anything other than his hand(s) or glove in it's
proper place.

CATCHER'S BOX. The catcher's box is an area defined by
lines which are considered within the catcher's box. The
catcher's body and equipment are considered within the
box unless touching the ground outside the box. The
catcher must remain in the box until:
A. (Fast Pitch Only) The pitch is released.
B. (Slow Pitch Only) The pitched ball is batted, touches
the ground or plate or reaches the catcher's box.

CHARGED CONFERENCE. A charged conference takes
place when:
A. **Defensive Conference**. The defensive team requests a
suspension of play for any reason, and a representative
(not on the field) enters the playing field and gives the
umpire cause to believe that he has delivered a mes-
sage (by any means) to the pitcher. When the manager crosses the foul line on the return to the dugout,
the conference is over.
B. **Offensive Conference**. The offensive team requests a
suspension of play to allow the manager or other team
representatives to confer with the batter and/or
runner(s).

CHOPPED BALL. (Slow Pitch Only) A chopped hit ball occurs when the batter strikes downward with a chopping motion of the bat so that the ball bounces high into the air.

COACH. A coach is a member of the team at bat who takes his place within one of the coach's boxes on the field to direct the players of his team in running the bases. Two coaches are allowed. One coach can have in his possession in the coach's box a score book, pen or pencil and an indicator, all of which shall be used for score keeping or record keeping purposes only. No communication equipment is allowed.

CROW HOP. (Fast Pitch Only) A crow hop is defined as the act of a pitcher who steps or hops off the front of the pitcher's plate, replants the pivot foot, establishing a second impetus (or starting point), pushes off from the newly established starting point and completes the delivery.

DEAD BALL. The ball is not in play and is not considered in play again until the pitcher has it in his possession and "play ball" has been declared by the umpire. A dead ball line is considered in play.

DEFENSIVE TEAM. The defensive team is the team in the field.

DISLODGED BASE. A dislodged base is a base displaced from its proper position.

DISQUALIFIED PLAYER. Refers to a player who violates the slow pitch home run rule and is disqualified for that game. A substitute can be entered for the disqualified player. If a team is shorthanded, they can continue to play one short. If two players short, the game is forfeited.

DOUBLE PLAY. A double play is a play by the defense resulting in two offensive players being legally put out.

EJECTION. The result of an incident which requires removal from the game by the umpire, whereby the ejected player or coach can no longer participate. A flagrant act will require the player or coach to leave the grounds for the remainder of the game. Any ejected player discovered participating will constitute a forfeit.

FAIR BALL. A fair ball is a batted ball that:
   A. Settles or is touched on or over fair territory between home and first base or between home and third base.
   B. Bounds over or past first or third base which is in fair territory, regardless of where the ball hits after going over the base.
   C. While on or over fair territory, touches the person, attached equipment or clothing of a player or an umpire.
   D. Touches first, second or third base.
   E. First falls or is first touched on or over fair territory beyond first, second or third base.
   F. While over fair territory, passes out of the playing field beyond the outfield fence.
   G. Hits the foul pole.
   NOTE: A batted ball shall be judged according to the relative position of the ball and the foul line, including the foul pole, and not as to whether the fielder is on fair or foul territory at the time he touches the ball. It does not matter whether the ball first touches fair or foul territory, as long as it does not touch anything foreign to the natural ground in foul territory and complies with all other aspects of a fair ball.

FAIR TERRITORY. Fair territory is that part of the playing field within, and including, the first and third base foul lines from home plate to the bottom of the playing field fence and perpendicularly upwards.

FAKE TAG. A form of obstruction by a fielder who neither has the ball nor is about to receive the ball, and which impedes the progress of a runner either advancing or returning to a base. The runner does not have to stop or slide. Merely slowing down when a fake tag is attempted would constitute obstruction.

FIELDER. A fielder is any player of the team in the field.

FLY BALL. A fly ball is any fair or foul ball batted into the air.

FORCE OUT. A force out is an out which may be made only when a runner loses the right to the base he is occupying because the batter becomes a batter-runner, and before the batter-runner or a succeeding runner has been put out. NOTE: If the forced runner, after touching the next base, retreats for any reason towards the base he had last occupied, the force play is reinstated and he may again be put out if the defense tags the runner or the base to which the runner is forced.

FOUL BALL. A foul ball is a batted ball that:
A. Settles or is touched on or over foul territory between home and first base or between home and third base.
B. Bounds or rolls past first or third base on or over foul territory.
C. While over foul territory, touches the person, attached equipment or clothing of a player or an umpire, or any object foreign to the natural ground.
D. First hits the ground or is first touched over foul territory beyond first or third base. A caught fly ball is not a foul ball.

E. Touches the batter or the bat in the batter's hand(s) a second time while the batter is within the batter's box.

FOUL TIP. A foul tip is a batted ball which goes directly from the bat, not higher than the batter's head, to the catcher's hand(s) or glove and is legally caught by the catcher. It is not a catch if it is a rebound unless the ball first touched the catcher's hand(s) or glove and does not touch the ground, batter or umpire.

HELMET.
   A. **Offensive:** All helmets must have double ear flaps and be approved by the National Operating Committee on Standards for Athletic Equipment (NOCSAE).
   B. **Defensive:** Any player may wear an approved helmet with or without earflaps. It must have a bill.
   C. **Catcher:** Skull helmets currently do not have NOCSAE standards.

HOME TEAM. The home team shall be designated by mutual agreement or by a flip of a coin, unless otherwise stated in the rules of the organization which the schedule of games is being played.

ILLEGAL BAT. An illegal bat is one that does not meet the requirements of Rule 3, Section 1. (For Illegal Warm-Up Bat, see Rule 3, Section 2)

ILLEGALLY BATTED BALL. An illegally batted ball occurs when the batter hits the ball fair or foul and:
   A. The entire foot is completely outside the lines of the batter's box and on the ground.
   B. Any part of the foot is touching home plate.
   C. An illegal or altered bat is used.

ILLEGAL PITCHER. A player legally in the game, but one who may not pitch as a result of being removed from the

pitching position by the umpire because of:
A. Two charged defensive conferences in one inning.
B. (Slow Pitch Only) Pitching or warming up with
   excessive speed after a warning.
   EFFECT: If an illegal pitcher returns to the pitching
   position and has thrown one pitch he is ejected from
   the game.

ILLEGAL SUBSTITUTE. A player who has entered the
game without reporting.

INELIGIBLE PLAYER. A player who does not meet the
requirements of ASA Code. The determination of
eligibility is not the responsibility of the umpire. The use
of an ineligible player will constitute a forfeit if properly
protested.

IN FLIGHT. In flight is the term used for any batted,
thrown or pitched ball which has not yet touched the
ground or some object or person other than a fielder.

IN JEOPARDY. In jeopardy is a term indicating that the
ball is in play and an offensive player may be put out.

INFIELD. The infield is that portion of the field in fair
territory which includes areas normally covered by
infielders.

INFIELD FLY. An infield fly is a fair fly ball (not including
a line drive or an attempted bunt) which can be caught
by an infielder with ordinary effort when first and second
bases or first, second and third bases are occupied before
two are out. Any defensive player who positions himself
in the infield at the start of the pitch shall be considered
an infielder for the purpose of this rule. The infield fly is
ruled when the ball reaches the highest point based on
the position of the closest infielder regardless who makes

the play. When it seems apparent that a batted ball will be an infield fly, the umpire shall immediately declare, "Infield Fly. The batter is out." for the benefit of the runners. If the ball is near a foul line, the umpire shall declare, "Infield Fly. The batter is out if fair."

The ball is alive and runners may advance at the risk of the ball being caught. The runner can tag up and advance once the batted ball is touched (prior to catching), the same as on any fly ball. If a declared infield fly becomes a foul ball, it is treated the same as any foul.

INNING. An inning is that portion of a game within which the teams alternate on offense and defense and in which there are three outs for each team. A new inning begins immediately after the final out of the previous inning.

INTERFERENCE. Interference is the act of an offensive player or team member which impedes or confuses a defensive player attempting to execute a play.

JUNIOR OLYMPIC PLAYER. Any player 18 years and under who has not reached their 19th birthday prior to September 1.
NOTE: If Junior Olympic players play on an adult team, it is considered playing in an adult league and adult rules will be in effect.

LEAPING. (Fast Pitch Only) An act by the pitcher which causes him to be airborne on his initial move and push from the pitcher's plate. The momentum built by the forward movement of the pitcher causes the entire body including both the pivot foot and the non-pivot foot to be in the air and moving toward home plate as the delivery is completed. With this style of pitching, the pitcher will release the ball simultaneously with his return to the ground. The pivot foot will then slide to the side and drag as the pitcher follows through or completes the delivery. This follow through should not be confused with replanting and gaining a second starting point (defined as the "crow hop"), but simply a finish or follow through of the leap style of pitching. At the completion of the leap, the non pivot foot is planted but will not allow the pitcher to gain further distance towards the plate, therefore the slide and drag of the pivot foot is a legal act.

LEGAL TOUCH. A legal touch occurs when a runner or batter-runner who is not touching a base is touched by the ball while it is securely held in a fielder's hand(s). The ball is not considered as having been securely held if it is juggled or dropped by the fielder after having touched the runner, unless the runner deliberately knocks the ball from the hand(s) of the fielder. It is sufficient for the runner to be touched with the glove or hand(s) holding the ball.

LINE DRIVE. A line drive is a fly ball that is batted sharply and directly into the playing field.

OBSTRUCTION. Obstruction is the act of:
   A. A defensive player or team member which hinders or prevents a batter from striking at or hitting a pitched ball.
   B. A fielder, who is not in possession of the ball, in the act of fielding a batted ball, nor about to receive a thrown ball, which impedes the progress of a runner or batter-runner who is legally running bases.

OFFENSIVE TEAM. The offensive team is the team at bat.

ON-DECK BATTER. The on-deck batter is the offensive player whose name follows the name of the batter in the batting order.

OUTFIELD. The outfield is that portion of the field in fair territory which is not normally covered by an infielder.

OVERSLIDE. An overslide is the act of an offensive player when, as a runner, he overslides a base he is attempting to reach. It is usually caused when his momentum causes him to lose contact with the base which then causes him to be in jeopardy. The batter-runner may overslide first base without being in jeopardy.

OVERTHROW. An overthrow occurs when a thrown ball from a fielder goes beyond the boundary lines of the playing field (dead ball territory) or becomes a blocked ball.

PASSED BALL. (Fast Pitch Only) A passed ball is a legally delivered ball that should have been held or controlled by the catcher with ordinary effort.

PIVOT FOOT. (Fast Pitch Only) The pivot foot is that foot which must remain in contact with the pitcher's plate. Pushing off with the pivot foot from a place other than the pitcher's plate is illegal. (Slow Pitch Only) The pivot foot is the foot which the pitcher must keep in constant contact with the pitcher's plate until the ball is released.

PLAY BALL. Play ball is the term used by the plate umpire to indicate that play shall start and shall not be declared until all defensive players are in fair territory except the catcher, who must be in the catcher's box.

PROTESTS. There are three types of protests:
   A. Misinterpretation of a playing rule—must be made before the next pitch or, if on the last play of the game, before the umpires leave the playing field.
   B. Illegal substitute or re-entry—must be made while they are in the game and before the umpires leave the playing field.

C. Ineligible player—can be made any time during the game or before the offending team's next game. Eligibility is the decision of the protest committee.

QUICK RETURN PITCH. A quick return pitch is one made by the pitcher with the obvious attempt to catch the batter off balance. This would be before the batter takes his desired position in the batter's box or while he is still off balance as a result of the previous pitch.

RUNNER. A runner is an offensive player who has reached first base and has not yet been put out.

SACRIFICE FLY. A sacrifice fly is scored when, with fewer than two outs, the batter scores a runner with a fly ball or line drive that is:
A. caught.
B. dropped by an outfielder (or an infielder running into the outfield), and, in the scorer's judgment, the runner could have scored after the catch had the fly ball or line drive been caught.

STARTING PITCHER. The player listed as a pitcher on the lineup card or official score book.

STARTING PLAYER. A starting player shall be official when the lineup is inspected and approved by the plate umpire and team manager at the pre-game meeting. The names may be entered on the official score sheet in advance of this meeting; however, changes can be made at the pre-game meeting with no charged substitutions.

STEALING. (Fast Pitch Only) Stealing is the act of a runner attempting to advance during a pitch to the batter.

STRIKE ZONE. When a batter assumes a natural batting stance, the strike zone is that space over any part of home plate between the batter's:

A. (Fast Pitch Only) Arm pits and the top of his knees.

B. (Slow Pitch Only) Back shoulder and his front knee.

TRAPPED CATCH. A trapped catch is (a) a batted fly ball or line drive which hits the ground or a fence prior to being caught, (b) a thrown ball to any base for a force out which is caught with the glove over the ball on the ground rather than under the ball, and (c) (Fast Pitch Only) a pitched ball which touches the ground on a strike prior to the catcher catching it.

TIME. Time is the term used by the umpire to order the suspension of play.

TRIPLE PLAY. A triple play is a continuous action play by the defense in which three offensive players are put out.

TURN AT BAT. A turn at bat begins when a player first enters the batter's box and continues until he is put out, becomes a batter-runner, or is substituted for while at bat.

WILD PITCH. (Fast Pitch Only) A wild pitch is a legally delivered ball that the catcher cannot catch or stop and control with ordinary effort.

RULE 2 - THE PLAYING FIELD

SECTION 1. The playing field is the area within which the ball may be legally played and fielded. There shall be a clear and unobstructed area between the foul lines and within the radius of the prescribed fence distances from home plate.

NOTE: If the base distances or the pitching distance is found to be at the wrong dimensions during the course of the game, correct the error, with no penalty, and continue playing the game. Every effort should be made by the umpire to obtain the correct dimensions.

SECTION 2. Ground or special rules establishing the limits of the playing field may be agreed upon by leagues or opposing teams whenever backstops, fences, stands, vehicles, spectators or other obstructions are within the prescribed area. Any obstruction on fair ground less than the prescribed fence distances from home plate should be clearly marked for the umpire's information.

If using a baseball field, the mound should be removed and the backstop distance must meet those prescribed (minimum of 25 feet [7.62m] or a maximum of 30 feet [9.14m] from home plate).

SECTION 3. For the layout of the diamond, refer to drawing showing official dimensions for a softball diamond. This section serves as an example for laying out a diamond with 60-foot bases and a 46-foot pitching distance.

To determine the position of home plate, draw a line in the direction desired to lay the diamond. Drive a stake at the corner of home plate nearest the catcher. Fasten a cord to this stake and tie knots, or otherwise mark the cord, at 46 feet (14.02m), 60 feet (18.29m), 84 feet 10

OFFICIAL DISTANCE TABLE (ADULT)

ADULT	DIVISION	BASES	PITCHING	MIN. FENCE	MAX. FENCE
Fast Pitch	Women	60' (18.29 m)	40' (12.19 m)	200' (60.96 m)	250' (76.20 m)*
	Men	60' (18.29 m)	46' (14.02 m)	225' (68.58 m)	250' (76.20 m)
	Jr. Men	60' (18.29 m)	46' (14.02 m)	225' (68.58 m)	250' (76.20 m)
Modified Pitch	Women	60' (18.29 m)	40' (12.19 m)	200' (60.96 m)	
	Men	60' (18.29 m)	46' (14.02 m)	265' (80.80 m)	
Slow Pitch	Women	65' (19.81 m)	50' (15.24 m)	265' (80.80 m)	275' (83.82 m)
	Men	65' (19.81 m)	50' (15.24 m)	275' (83.82 m)	315' (96.01 m)*
	Coed	65' (19.81 m)	50' (15.24 m)	275' (83.82 m)	300' (91.44 m)
	Super	65' (19.81 m)	50' (15.24 m)	300' (91.44 m)	325' (99.08 m)
16-Inch Pitch	Women	55' (16.76 m)	38' (11.58 m)	200' (60.96 m)	200' (60.96 m)
	Men	55' (16.76 m)	38' (11.58 m)	250' (76.20 m)	

* Effective 1996

1/4 inches (25.86m), and at 120 feet (36.58m). Place the cord (without stretching) along the direction line and place a stake at the 46-foot (14.02m) marker. This will be the front line at the middle of the pitcher's plate. Along the same line, drive a stake at the 84-foot 10 1/4-inch (25.68m) marker. This will be the center of second base. Place the 120-foot (36.58m) marker at the center of second base and, taking hold of the cord at the 60-foot (18.29m) marker, walk to the right of the direction line until the cord is taut and drive a stake at the 60-foot (18.29m) marker. This will be the outside corner of first base and the cord will now form the lines to first and second bases. Again, holding the cord at the 60-foot (18.29m) marker, walk across the field and, in like manner, mark the outside corner of third base. Home plate, first base, and third base are wholly inside the diamond. To check the diamond, place the home plate end of the cord at the first base stake and the 120-foot (36.58m) marker at third base. The 60-foot (18.29m) marker should now check at home plate and second base.

In the layout of a 65-foot base path diamond, follow the same procedure with the following substitute dimensions: 65 foot (19.81m), 130 foot (39.62m), and 91 feet 11 inches (28.07m). Check all distances with a steel tape whenever possible.

A. The three-foot (0.91m) line is drawn parallel to and three feet (0.91m) from the baseline, starting at a point halfway between home plate and first base.

B. The batter's on-deck circle is a five-foot (1.52m) circle (2½-foot [0.76m] radius) placed adjacent to the end of the players' bench or dugout area closest to home plate.

C. The batter's box, one on each side of home plate shall measure three feet (0.91m) by seven feet (2.13m). The inside lines of the batter's box shall be six inches

OFFICIAL DISTANCE TABLE (YOUTH)

YOUTH	DIVISION	BASES	PITCHING	MIN. FENCE	MAX. FENCE
Fast Pitch	G10-U	55' (16.76 m)	35' (10.67 m)	150' (45.72 m)	175' (53.34 m)
	G12-U	60' (18.29 m)	35' (10.67 m)	175' (53.34 m)	200' (60.96 m)
	G14-U	60' (18.29 m)	40' (12.19 m)	175' (53.34 m)	200' (60.96 m)
	G16-U	60' (18.29 m)	40' (12.19 m)	200' (60.96 m)	225' (68.58 m)
	G18-U	60' (18.29 m)	40' (12.19 m)	200' (60.96 m)	225' (68.58 m)
	B10-U	55' (16.76 m)	35' (10.67 m)	150' (45.72 m)	175' (53.34 m)
	B12-U	60' (18.29 m)	40' (12.19 m)	175' (53.34 m)	200' (60.96 m)
	B14-U	60' (18.29 m)	46' (14.02 m)	175' (53.34 m)	200' (60.96 m)
	B16-U	60' (18.29 m)	46' (14.02 m)	200' (60.96 m)	225' (68.58 m)
	B18-U	60' (18.29 m)	46' (14.02 m)	200' (60.96 m)	225' (68.58 m)
Slow Pitch	G10-U	55' (16.76 m)	35' (10.67 m)	150' (45.72 m)	175' (53.34 m)
	G12-U	60' (18.29 m)	40' (12.19 m)	175' (53.34 m)	200' (60.96 m)
	G14-U	65' (19.81 m)	46' (14.02 m)	225' (68.58 m)	250' (76.20 m)
	G16-U	65' (19.81 m)	50' (15.24 m)	225' (68.58 m)	250' (76.20 m)
	G18-U	65' (19.81 m)	50' (15.24 m)	225' (68.58 m)	250' (76.20 m)
	B10-U	55' (16.76 m)	35' (10.67 m)	150' (45.72 m)	175' (53.34 m)
	B12-U	60' (18.29 m)	40' (12.19 m)	175' (53.34 m)	200' (60.96 m)
	B14-U	65' (19.81 m)	46' (14.02 m)	250' (76.20 m)	275' (83.82 m)
	B16-U	65' (19.81 m)	50' (15.24 m)	275' (83.82 m)	300' (91.44 m)
	B18-U	65' (19.81 m)	50' (15.24 m)	275' (83.82 m)	300' (91.44 m)

(15.24cm) from home plate. The front line of the box shall be four feet (1.22m) in front of a line drawn through the center of home plate. The lines are considered as being within the batter's box.

D. The catcher's box shall be 10 feet (3.05m) in length from the rear outside corners of the batters' boxes and shall be eight feet, five inches (2.57m) wide.

E. Each coach's box is behind a line 15 feet (4.57m) long drawn outside the diamond. The line is parallel to and eight feet (2.44m) from the first and third base line, extended from the bases toward home plate.

F. The pitcher's plate shall be of rubber or wood, 24 inches (60.96cm) long and six inches (15.24cm) wide. The top of the plate shall be level with the ground. The front of the plate shall be the prescribed pitching distances from the back point of the plate. It shall be permanently attached to the ground at distances indicated in Rule 2, Section 1. (Fast Pitch Only) There shall be a 16-foot (4.88m) circle, eight feet (2.44m) in radius, drawn from the center of the pitcher's plate. The lines drawn around the pitcher's plate are considered inside the circle.

G. Home plate shall be made of rubber or other suitable material. It shall be a five-sided figure, 17 inches (43.18cm) wide across the edge facing the pitcher. The sides shall be parallel to the inside lines of the batter's box and shall be 8½ inches (21.59cm) long. The sides of the point facing the catcher shall be 12 inches (30.48cm) long.

   1. (Senior Men's Slow Pitch) The second home plate shall be placed eight feet from the back tip of home plate on an extended line from first base. A line shall be drawn from third base to the second home plate. (See diagram.)

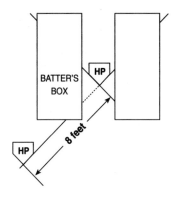

H. The bases, other than home plate, shall be 15 inches
   (38.10cm) square, shall be made of canvas or other
   suitable material and not more than five inches
   (12.70cm) in thickness. The bases should be properly
   fastened in position.

   1. The double base is approved for use at first
      base. This base is 15 by 30 inches and made of
      canvas or other suitable material. Half the base
      is white (over fair territory) and half is orange
      (over foul territory). It should not be more than
      five inches (12.70cm) in thickness.

      NOTE: When using the double base at first, the
      following rules should be enforced:

      a. A batted ball hitting the white portion is
         declared fair and a batted ball hitting the
         orange portion is declared foul.

      b. Whenever a play is being made on the
         batter-runner, the defense must use the
         white portion and the batter-runner the
         orange portion. On extra base hits or balls
         hit to the outfield when there is no play

being made at the double base, the runner may touch the white or orange portion.

c. (Fast Pitch Only) On a dropped third strike, the batter-runner and the defensive player may use either the orange or the white portion.

d. The batter-runner must use the orange portion on the first attempt at first base; however, should he reach and go beyond first base, he must return to the white portion.

e. Should the batter-runner round the base on a hit to the infield or the outfield, he must return to the white portion.

f. When tagging up on a fly ball, the white portion must be used.

g. (Fast Pitch & 16-Inch Slow Pitch Only) On an attempted pick-off play, the runner must return to the white portion.

2. (Senior Men's Slow Pitch) The double first base shall be used in this division of play.

RULE 3 - EQUIPMENT

SECTION 1. THE OFFICIAL BAT.

A. Shall be made of one piece of hardwood, or formed from a block of wood consisting of two or more pieces of wood bonded together with an adhesive in such a way that the grain direction of all pieces is essentially parallel to the length of the bat.

B. Shall be metal, plastic, graphite, carbon, magnesium, fiberglass, ceramic or any other composite material approved by the ASA. Any new composite construction bat must be reviewed and approved by the ASA.

C. May be laminated but must contain only wood or adhesive and have a clear finish (if finished).

D. Shall be round or three-sided and shall be smooth. If the barrel end has a knurled finish the maximum surface roughness is no more than 250 if measured by a profilometer or 4/1000 if measured by a spectrograph.

E. Shall not be more than 34 inches (87.0cm) long, nor exceed 38 ounces (1100.0g) in weight.

F. If round, shall not be more than 2¼ inches (6.0cm) in diameter at its largest part; and if three-sided, shall not exceed 2¼ inches (6.0cm) on the hitting surface. A tolerance of ½₂ inch (0.90mm) is permitted to allow for expansion on the round bat.
    NOTE: If the bat ring goes over the bat it should be considered a legal bat.

G. If metal, may be angular.

H. Shall not have exposed rivets, pins, rough or sharp edges or any form of exterior fastener that would present a hazard. A metal bat shall be free of burrs.

I. If metal, shall not have a wooden handle.

J. Shall have a safety grip of cork, tape (no smooth, plastic tape) or composition material. The safety grip shall not be less than 10 inches (25.0cm) long and shall not extend more than 15 inches (40.0cm) from the small end of the bat. Any molded finger-formed grip made by the bat manufacturer, if used, must be permanently attached to the bat or attached to the bat with safety tape and must be approved by the Equipment Standards Committee. Resin, pine tar or spray substances placed on the safety grip to enhance the grip are permissible on the grip only. Tape applied to any bat must be continuously spiral. It does not have to be a solid layer of tape. It may not exceed two layers. Taping of a bat less than the required length is considered illegal.

K. If metal, and not made of one-piece construction with the barrel end closed, shall have a rubber or vinyl plastic or other approved material insert firmly secured at the large end of the bat.

L. Shall have a safety knob of a minimum of ⅛ inch protruding at a 90-degree angle from the handle. It may be molded, lathed, welded or permanently fastened. A "flare" or "cone" grip attached to the bat will be considered altered. The knob may be taped as long as there is no violation of this section. (See page 00.)

M. Shall be marked OFFICIAL SOFTBALL by the manufacturer. If the words OFFICIAL SOFTBALL cannot be read due to wear and tear on the bat, the bat should be declared legal if it is legal in all other aspects.
NOTE: Softball bats used in ASA championship tournament play must be approved by the Equipment Standards Committee. Manufacturers must submit all new designed bats to the ASA Equipment Standards Committee for approval prior to sales.

SECTION 2. WARM-UP BATS.

No more than two official softball bats, one ASA approved warm-up bat or a combination of the two, not to exceed two, may be used by the on-deck batter in the on-deck circle. The warm-up bat should meet the following requirements to be approved:

A. Stamped with ¼ inch letters WB on either end of the bat or marked in one-inch letters the words WARM-UP BAT only on the barrel end of the bat.

B. A minimum weight of 48 ounces (1360.0g).

C. A minimum barrel diameter of 2½ inches (6.0m).

D. Shall have a safety grip of at least 10 inches (25.0cm) and no more than 15 inches (40.0cm) extended from the knob.

E. Be of one-piece construction or a one-piece permanently assembled bat approved by the Equipment Standards Committee.

NOTE: For approved equipment list, see page 32.

SECTION 3. THE OFFICIAL SOFTBALL.

A. Shall be a regular, smooth-seamed, flat-surfaced, pebble-textured (Slow Pitch Only) or dimple-textured ball with concealed stitches.

B. Shall have a center core made of either No. 1 quality long fiber kapok, a mixture of cork and rubber, a polyurethane mixture or other materials approved by the ASA.

C. May be hand or machine-wound with a fine quality twisted yarn and covered with latex or rubber cement.

D. Shall have a cover cemented to the ball by application of cement to the underside of the cover and sewn with waxed thread of cotton or linen. If the cover is molded, it may be bonded to the core or be of the same composition as the core. Either molded type must have an authentic facsimile of stitching as approved by the ASA.

E. Shall have a cover of chrome-tanned, top-grain horsehide or cowhide, synthetic material or other materials approved by the ASA.

F. The 12-inch (30.0cm) ball shall be between 11⅞ inches (30.0cm) and 12⅛ inches (31.0cm) in circumference and shall weigh between 6¼ ounces (180.0g) and seven ounces (200.0g). The smooth-seamed style shall not have fewer than 88 stitches in each cover, sewn by the two-needle method, or with an authentic facsimile of stitching as approved by the ASA.

G. The 11-inch (27.0cm) ball shall be between 10⅞ inches (27.0cm) and 11⅛ inches (28.0cm) in circumference. It shall weigh between 5⅞ ounces (165.0g) and 6¼ ounces (175.0g). The smooth-seamed style shall not have fewer than 80 stitches in each cover, sewn by the two-needle method, or with an authentic facsimile of stitching as approved by the ASA.

H. The white-stitch 12-inch ball with a COR of .50 or under shall be used in the following ASA play: men's and women's fast pitch, boys and girls 12-, 14-, 16-, and 18-under fast pitch, and boys 14-, 16-, and 18-under slow pitch.

I. The white-stitch 11-inch ball with a COR of .50 or under shall be used in the following ASA play: boys and girls 10-under fast pitch.

J. The red-stitch (and/or red indelible stamping as approved by the ASA) 12-inch ball with a COR of .47 and under shall be used in the following ASA play: men's slow pitch and coed (male batters only) slow pitch. It must be marked MSP- 47.
NOTE: The .50 COR yellow optic, red-stitch ball is not legal for slow pitch play.

K. The red-stitch (and/or red indelible stamping as

OFFICIAL SOFTBALL MEASUREMENTS

SOFTBALL	THREAD COLOR	MIN. SIZE	MAX. SIZE	MIN. WEIGHT	MAX. WEIGHT	MARKING
12" FP (30.0cm)	white	11⅞ in. 30.0cm	12⅛ in. 31.0cm	6¼ oz 180.0g	7 oz 200.0g	ASA Logo
12" SP (30.0cm)	red	11⅞ in. 30.0cm	12⅛ in. 31.0cm	6¼ oz 180.0g	7 oz 200.0g	MSP-47 ASA Logo
16" SP (41.0cm)	white	15⅞ in 40.9cm	16⅛ in 41.0cm	9 oz 225.0g	10 oz 283.0g	ASA Logo
11" SP (27.0 cm)	red	10⅞ in 27.0cm	11⅛ in. 28.0cm	5⅞ oz 165.0g	6⅛ oz 175.0g	GWSP-47 ASA Logo
11" FP (27.0 cm)	white	10⅞ in 27.0cm	11⅛ in 28.0cm	5⅞ oz 165.0g	6⅛ oz 175.0g	ASA Logo

approved by the ASA) 11-inch ball with a COR of .47
and under shall be used in the following ASA play:
women's slow pitch, coed slow pitch (women batters
only), boys 10- and 12-under slow pitch and girls 12-,
14-, 16-, and 18-under slow pitch. It must be marked
GWSP-47.

EFFECT - J-K: If the wrong ball is used, the manager
of the offensive team has the option of taking the
result of the play or having the last batter rebat and
assume the ball and strike count prior to the wrong
ball being discovered.

L. The gold stitch 12-inch ball with a COR of .44 and
under shall be used in the super slow pitch division

M. Softballs used in ASA play must meet standards set by
the ASA as shown on the chart and **must be stamped
with the ASA logo.**

SECTION 4. GLOVES may be worn by any player, but
mitts may be used only by the catcher and first baseman.
No top lacing, webbing or other device between the
thumb and body of the glove or mitt worn by a first
baseman or catcher, or a glove worn by any fielder; shall
be more than five inches (12.70cm) in length. (Fast Pitch
Only) The pitcher's glove shall not be partially or one
solid color of white or gray.

**SECTION 5. MASKS, BODY PROTECTORS, SHIN
GUARDS AND HELMETS.**
   A. (Fast Pitch Only) Adult catchers must wear masks
      with throat protectors. An extended wire protector
      may be worn in lieu of an attached throat protector.
   B. (Slow Pitch Only) Junior Olympic catchers must wear
      an approved batter's helmet with ear flaps, or the
      catcher's helmet and mask.
   C. (Fast Pitch Only) Junior Olympic catchers must wear

a mask with throat protector, approved helmet with ear flaps, shin guards which offer protection to the knee caps and body protector. An extended wire protector may be worn in lieu of an attached throat protector.

NOTE: Any player warming up a Junior Olympic pitcher must wear a mask with throat protector and approved helmet with ear flaps.

D. **HELMETS.**

    1. **OFFENSE.** All adult fast pitch, modified pitch and Junior Olympic fast and slow pitch offensive players, including the on-deck batter and Junior Olympic players acting as coaches in the coach's box, must properly wear NOCSAE-approved batting helmets. Helmets must be NOCSAE approved.

    EFFECT: Failure to wear the batting helmet when ordered to do so by the umpire shall cause the player to be ejected from the game. Wearing the helmet improperly or removing the helmet during a live ball play and judged by the umpire to be a deliberate act shall cause the violator to be declared out immediately. The ball remains alive.

    NOTE: Calling a runner out for removing a helmet does not remove force play situations. Umpires should use discretion as to the intent of the rule concerning player safety.

    2. **DEFENSE.** Any defensive player may wear an approved helmet of similar color as the team caps.

SECTION 6. UNIFORM.

All players on a team shall properly wear uniforms that are alike in color, trim and style. If because of the blood rule a change is required and the uniform part does not match, the player will not be penalized. Coaches must be neatly attired and dressed alike or in team uniform and in accordance with the color code of the team. All protective equipment should be worn properly.

NOTE: If a player is requested by the umpire to remove jewelry, illegal shoes or illegal parts of the uniform and they refuse, the player will not be allowed to play.

A. **HEADWEAR.**
1. (Fast Pitch Male) Ball caps are mandatory and must be alike.
2. (Female Fast Pitch & All Slow Pitch) Ball caps, visors and headbands are optional for players. Players are not required to wear headwear, but if worn, all headwear must be of the same type (i.e., all caps, visors or headbands). Handkerchiefs do not qualify as headbands and cannot be worn around the head or neck.
NOTE: Plastic visors are not allowed.
B. **PANTS/SLIDING PANTS.** All players' pants shall be either all long or all short in style. Players may wear a solid-colored pair of sliding pants. It is not mandatory that all players wear sliding pants, but if more than one player wears them, they must be alike in color and style. No player may wear ragged, frayed or slit legs on exposed sliding pants.
C. **UNDERSHIRTS.** Players may wear a solid-colored undershirt (it may be white). It is not mandatory that all players wear an undershirt, but if more than one player wears one, those that are worn must be alike. No player may wear ragged, frayed or slit sleeves on exposed undershirts.

D. **NUMBERS.** An Arabic number of contrasting color
at least six inches (15.24cm) high must be worn on
the back of all uniform shirts. No players on the same
team may wear identical numbers. (Numbers 3 and
03 are examples of identical numbers.) Players without numbers will not be permitted to play. If duplicate numbers exist, only one of the players may play
at a time. There is no penalty for a player wearing a
wrong number. Correct the number in the scorebook
and continue play.

NOTE: There is no penalty for duplicate numbers.
Just ask one player to change jerseys, or require a substitute to enter for one of the players.

E. **CASTS.** Plaster or other hard substances in their final
form may not be worn during the game. Any exposed
metal may be considered legal if covered by soft
material and taped.

F. **JEWELRY.** Exposed jewelry, which is judged by the
umpire to be dangerous, must be removed and may
not be worn during the game.

NOTE: Medical alert bracelets or necklaces are not
considered jewelry. If worn, they must be taped to the
body so as to remain visible.

G. **SHOES.** must be worn by all players. A shoe shall be
considered official if it is made with either canvas or
leather uppers or similar material(s). The soles may be
either smooth or have soft or hard rubber cleats.
Ordinary metal sole or heel plates may be used if the
spikes on the plates do not extend more than ¾ of an
inch (1.91cm) from the sole or heel of the shoe. Shoes
with round metal spikes are illegal. No shoes with
detachable cleats that screw ON are allowed; however,
shoes with detachable cleats that screw INTO the shoe
are allowed. Junior Olympic/Coed/Men's Senior Play:

No metal spikes nor hard plastic or polyurethane spikes similar to metal sole and heel plates are allowed.

SECTION 7. ALL EQUIPMENT.

Notwithstanding the foregoing, the ASA reserves the right to withhold or withdraw approval of any equipment which, in the ASA's sole determination, significantly changes the character of the game, affects the safety of participants or spectators, or renders a player's performance more a product of his equipment rather than his individual skill.

TYPES OF APPROVED EQUIPMENT

Warm-up Bats: All-Star, Bratt's Bat, Dirx dX250 (Dirx Company), Dudley, Hillerich & Bradsby (Louisville Slugger), Whip-O, Meiga bat, Sledge Hammer (Steele's Sports), Swingmaster (J. deBeer), TopHand (Switch-Hitter, Inc.) and Worth.

Grips: Power Pad, Trigger-Grip, Rotary Grip, Bear Grip and Dome Style Power Grip are all approved.

RULE 4 - PLAYERS AND SUBSTITUTES

SECTION 1. PLAYERS.

A. A team must have the required number of players present in the team area to start or continue a game. Players listed in the starting lineup and not available at game time may be substituted for and re-entered later.

1. Official lineup cards are to be completed and submitted to the official scorer or umpire at the start of each game. The lineup shall contain the first and last name, position and uniform number of each player.
   NOTE: If a wrong number is on the lineup sheet, correct it and continue playing with no penalty.

2. All available substitutes should be listed in the designated place by their last name, first name and uniform number.

3. Eligible roster members may be added to the available substitute list at any time during the game.

B. Male rosters shall include only male players and female rosters shall include only female players.

C. A team shall consist of players in the following positions:

1. Fast Pitch. Nine players - pitcher (F1), catcher (F2), first baseman (F3), second baseman (F4), third baseman (F5), shortstop (F6), left fielder (F7), center fielder (F8) and right fielder (F9).

2. Fast Pitch with a Designated Player (DP). Ten players - same as fast pitch plus a DP.
   NOTE: Refer to Section 3 DESIGNATED PLAYER for options resulting in nine players

continuing the game.

3. Slow Pitch. Ten players - same as fast pitch plus an extra fielder (F10).

4. Slow Pitch With An Extra Player (EP). Eleven players - same as slow pitch plus an EP who bats in the lineup. Seniors may have 11 or 12 players using one or two EP's.

5. Coed. Ten players, five male and five female - same as slow pitch with the following positioning requirements: two males and two females in both the infield and the outfield, and one male and one female as pitcher and/or catcher.

6. Coed With Extra Players (EP). Twelve players, six male and six female - same as coed plus two EPs who bat in the lineup.

7. A physically challenged player can play as a defensive player only (DEFO). (See Section 2)

D. SHORT-HANDED RULE.

This rule may be used with the following requirements:

1. If a team begins play with the required number of players as listed in C above, that team may continue a game with one less player than it started with (slow pitch) or one less player than is currently in the game (fast pitch), whenever a player leaves the game for any reason other than ejection.

2. If the player leaving the game is a runner, he shall be declared out.

3. When the player who has left the game is scheduled to bat, an out shall be declared for each turn at bat.

4. The player who has left the game cannot return to the lineup.

EXCEPTION: A player who has left the game under the blood rule (Rule 4, Section 8 C) may return.

EFFECT - Section 1 A-D: The game is forfeited for any violation of requirements.

SECTION 2. AMERICAN DISABILITY ACT RULE
(Slow Pitch Only)

A. This rule may be used for a person(s) who is physically challenged as determined by the American Disabilities Act passed on July 25, 1990. As a result of the player's disability, he can play either offense or defense.

B. Teams using a physically challenged player on either offense or defense only must have 11 players. If the physically challenged player can play both, only 10 players are needed.

C. When a physically challenged person plays offense only, the team will follow the EP ruling as written. There would be 11 hitters including the ADA player, and only 10 who play defense.

D. When a physically challenged player plays defense only, they will be listed as the DEFO and placed last in the lineup. The team has the option to bat 10 or 11 players (if the EP is also used). When using a DEFO, it must be made known prior to the start of the game.

E. If a team starts the game with the DEFO option, the DEFO can never play offense. If this person for any reason cannot continue to play and the team has no other physically challenged player for a substitute, the EP can now play in his defensive position.

F. The DEFO position has the same re-entry status as any other starting position as long as the person substituted is also determined to be physically challenged under the ADA program. The original DEFO may re-enter only in the same spot on the lineup sheet.

G. If a DEFO or DEFOS, one male and/or one female, is used in the coed division, the name(s) must be inserted at the end of the lineup. The EP or two EPs can be listed anywhere in the first 10 positions. The batting order must still alternate as outlined in Rule 7, Section 2D and the defensive positioning remains as outlined in Rule 4, Section 1C.

NOTE: This special rule has been adopted to accommodate the athlete who is physically challenged. The intent is not to change the game and/or not to deprive any player from playing who would normally play, therefore, when using the EP, the normal EP rules will be followed including substitutions and re-entry. If the EP is used in addition to the DEFO, the DEFO must play defense and any of the other 11 players will be eligible to play defense. Only 11 are allowed to bat.

SECTION 3. DESIGNATED PLAYER (Fast Pitch Only)

A. A designated player (DP) may be used for any player provided it is made known prior to the start of the game and his name is indicated on the lineup or score sheet as one of the nine hitters in the batting order.

B. The name of the player for whom the DP is batting (DEFO) will be placed in the 10th position in the scorebook.

C. The starting player listed as the DP must remain in the same position in the batting order for the entire game. The DP and his substitute, or the substitute's replacement, may never play offense at the same time.

D. The DP may be substituted for at any time, either by a pinch-hitter, pinch-runner or the defensive player for whom he is hitting (DEFO). If the starting DP is replaced on offense by the DEFO or by a substitute, the DP is considered to have left the game and he may re-enter one time, as long as he returns to his original position in the batting order.

    1. If replaced by the person playing defense only (DEFO), this reduces the number of players from 10 to nine. If the DP does not re-enter, the game may legally end with nine players.

    2. If the DP re-enters and the DEFO was batting in his spot, the DEFO can return to the number 10 position and play defense only or leave the game.

E. The DP may play defense at any position. Should the DP play defense for a player other than the one for whom he is batting (DEFO), that player will continue to bat but not play defense, and is not considered to have left the game. The DP may play defense for the DEFO and the DEFO is considered to have left the game, reducing the number of players from 10 to nine.

F. The person being batted for (DEFO) may be substituted for at any time, either by a legal substitute or the DP for whom he is playing defense. The DEFO may re-enter the game one time, either in the number 10 position or in the DP's position in the batting order.

    1. If returning to the number 10 position, he will again play defense only but may play any defensive position.

    2. If the DEFO returns to the DP's position, he will play offense and defense; there will be only nine players in the batting order.

G. Placing the defensive player only (DEFO) into one of the first nine positions for someone other than the original DP is considered an illegal re-entry. The manager and the DEFO are ejected.

EFFECT: Re-entering the DP into a batting position other than his original position is considered an illegal re-entry.

SECTION 4. EXTRA PLAYER (Slow Pitch Only).

A. An extra player (EP) is optional, but if one is used, it must be made known prior to the start of the game and be listed on the scoring sheet in the regular batting order. If the EP is used, he must be used the entire game. Failure to complete the game with 11 batters as a result of an ejected player, results in a forfeiture of the game.

B. The EP must remain in the same position in the batting order for the entire game.

C. If an EP is used, all 11 must bat and any 10 may play defense. Defensive positions may be changed, but the batting order must remain the same.

D. The EP may be substituted for at any time. The substitute must be a player who has not yet been in the game. The starting EP may re-enter.

E. If the EP is used in coed, all 12 must bat and any 10, (five male and five female), may play defense. Defensive positions may be changed as long as the coed positioning is followed. The batting order must remain the same throughout the game.

F. (Men's Senior Only). One or two extra players may be designated at any place in the batting order. The EP(s) may enter a game on defense at any time, but the batting order must remain the same throughout the game.

SECTION 5. RE-ENTRY.

A. Any of the starting players, including a DP (Fast Pitch Only) or an EP (Slow Pitch Only), may be substituted and re-entered once, provided players occupy the same batting positions whenever in the lineup. The starting player and the substitute(s) may not be in the lineup at the same time. If a manager removes a substitute from the game and re-enters the same substitute later in the game, this is considered an illegal re-entry.

B. Violation of re-entry rule is handled as a protest when brought to the attention of the umpire by the offended team and may be made anytime during the game. The protest need not be made prior to the next pitch.

EFFECT - Section 5 A-B: Both the manager and illegal player are ejected. All play that occurred while the illegal re-entry was in the game will stand.

NOTE: If the re-entry violation also violates the unreported substitute ruling, those penalties would also be in effect.

C. A starting player removed from the pitching position by the umpire and substituted for can re-enter the game at another position, but cannot return to the pitching position.

EFFECT: If an illegal pitcher returns to the pitching position and has thrown one pitch he is ejected from the game.

NOTE: This is not considered a re-entry violation so the manager is not ejected.

SECTION 6. SUBSTITUTES.

A substitute may take the place of a player whose name is in his team's batting order. The following regulations govern player substitutions:

A. The manager or team representative of the team making the substitution shall immediately notify the plate umpire at the time a substitute enters. The plate umpire shall then report the change to the scorer prior to the next pitch. If the violation is discovered prior to a pitch being made (legal or illegal), there is no penalty and the illegal substitute shall be declared legal.

B. Substitute players will be considered in the game when reported to the plate umpire. A player will not violate the substitution rule until one legal or illegal pitch has been thrown. The use of an illegal substitute is handled as a protest by the offended team. If the team manager or player in violation informs the umpire prior to the offended team's protest, there is no violation regardless of how long the player or players were illegally in the game.

1. **OFFENSE.** If the illegal player is discovered by the defense before the offensive manager, coach or player in violation informs the umpire and:

    (a) after one legal or illegal pitch has been thrown while he is at bat, he is ejected and a legal substitute assumes the ball and strike count. Any advance of runners while the illegal batter is at bat is legal.

    (b) he has completed his turn at bat and prior to the next legal or illegal pitch, or before the defensive team has left the field, the illegal player is called out, ejected and any advance of runners as a result of obstruction, an error, a hit batter or a dropped third strike (Fast Pitch), a walk, or a base hit is nullified.

    (c) he has completed his turn at bat and after the next legal or illegal pitch, or after the defensive team has left the field, the illegal player is ejected and any advance by runners while the illegal batter was at bat is legal.

2. **DEFENSE.** If the illegal player is discovered by the offense before the defensive manager, coach or player in violation informs the umpire and:

    (a) after he makes a play and prior to the next legal or illegal pitch, or before the defensive team has left the field, the offensive team has the option of taking the result of the play or having the last batter return and assume the ball and strike count he had prior to the discovery of the illegal player with each runner returning to the base at which he was prior to the play. The illegal player is ejected.

(b) after a legal or illegal pitch to the next batter, all play stands but the illegal player is ejected.

C. Any player may be removed from the game during any dead ball.

NOTE: The pitcher no longer has to pitch until the first batter facing him has completed his turn at bat or the side has been retired.

SECTION 7. EJECTED PLAYER.

A player or coach who has been ejected from the game is restricted to the bench unless the act is determined to be flagrant, when the player or coach must leave the grounds. Any ejected player discovered participating will constitute a forfeit.

SECTION 8. BLOOD RULE.

A player, coach or umpire who is bleeding or who has blood on his uniform shall be prohibited from participating further in the game until appropriate treatment can be administered. If medical care or treatment is administered in a reasonable length of time, the individual will not have to leave the game. The length of time that is considered reasonable is left to the umpire's judgment. Uniform rule violations will not be enforced if a uniform change is required. The umpire shall:

A. Stop the game and allow treatment if the injured

   player would affect the continuation of the game.
B. Immediately call a coach, trainer or other authorized
   person to the injured player.
C. Apply the rules of the game regarding substitution,
   short-handed player and re-entry if necessary.

RULE 5 - THE GAME

SECTION 1. HOME TEAM.

The team designated as home team shall bat last in the inning.

SECTION 2. FITNESS OF THE GROUND.

The fitness of the ground for a game shall be decided solely by the plate umpire.

SECTION 3. REGULATION GAME.

A. A regulation game shall consist of seven innings. A full seven innings need not be played if the team second at bat scores more runs in six and one-half innings and/or before the third out in the last of the seventh inning, or the run ahead rule is applied.

B. A game that is tied at the end of seven innings shall be continued by playing additional innings until one side has scored more runs than the other at the end of a complete inning, or until the team second at bat has scored more runs in their half of the inning before the third out is made.

C. A game called by the umpire shall be regulation if five or more complete innings have been played, or if the team second at bat has scored more runs in four or more innings than the other team has scored in five or more innings. The umpire is empowered to call a game at any time because of darkness, rain, fire, panic or other causes which place the patrons or players in peril. (For ASA national tournament play, see ASA Code 209 B)

D. Games that are not considered regulation shall be resumed at the exact point where they were stopped.

E. A regulation tie game shall be declared if the score is equal when the game is called at the end of five or

more complete innings, or if the team second at bat
has equaled the score of the first team at bat in the
incomplete inning.

F. Games that are regulation tie games shall be resumed
at the exact point where they were stopped.

SECTION 4. FORFEITED GAMES.

A forfeited game shall be declared by the umpire in favor
of the team not at fault in the following cases:

A. If an umpire is physically attacked by any team member and/or spectator.

B. If a team fails to appear on the field, or, being on the
field, refuses to begin a game for which it is scheduled
or assigned within a time set for forfeitures by the
organization which the team represents.

C. If one side refuses to continue to play after the game
has begun, unless the game has been suspended or terminated by the umpire.

D. If, after play has been suspended by the umpire, one
side fails to resume playing within two minutes after
"play ball" has been declared by the umpire.

E. If a team employs tactics noticeably designed to delay
or to hasten the game.

F. If, after warning by the umpire, any one of the rules
of the game is willfully violated.

G. If the order for the ejection of a player is not obeyed
within one minute.

H. If the ejection of a player or players from the game
results in fewer than the required number of players
to continue the game.

SECTION 5. SCORING OF RUNS.

A. One run shall be scored each time a runner legally
touches first, second or third bases and home plate
before the third out of an inning.

B. No run shall be scored if the third out of the inning is the result of:

1. A batter-runner being called out prior to reaching first base or any other runner forced out due to the batter becoming a batter runner.
2. A runner being put out by a tag or live ball appeal play prior to the lead runner touching home plate.
3. A preceding runner is declared out on an appeal play.
   NOTE: An appeal can be made after the third out in order to nullify a run.

SECTION 6. GAME WINNER.

The winner of the game shall be the team that scores more runs in a regulation game.

A. The score of a called regulation game shall be the score at the end of the last complete inning, unless the team second at bat has scored an equal number or more runs than the first team at bat in the incomplete inning. In this case, the score shall be that of the incomplete inning.
B. The score of a regulation tie game shall be the tie score when the game was terminated.
C. The score of a forfeited game shall be seven to zero in favor of the team not at fault.

SECTION 7. CHARGED CONFERENCE.

A. **Offensive Conference.** There shall be only one charged conference between the manager and/or other team representative(s) and the batter or runner(s) in an inning. The umpire shall not permit any such conferences in excess of one in an inning.
EFFECT: Ejection of the manager or coach who insists on another charged conference.

B. **Defensive Conference.** There shall be only one charged conference between the manager or other team representative from the dugout with each pitcher in an inning.

EFFECT: The second charged conference shall result in the removal of the pitcher from the pitching position for the remainder of the game.

PENALTY: If the pitcher returns to the pitcher's position at any time during the game after two defensive conferences in the same inning, he is ejected from the game. The removed pitcher can play another position on defense but cannot pitch again. If the removed player does re-enter to pitch again, he is ejected from the game.

SECTION 8. HOME RUN CLASSIFICATION (Slow Pitch Only). (Code Article 209 I)

A limit of over-the-fence home runs will be used in all men's and coed slow pitch divisions. All balls hit over the fence by a team in excess of the following limitations per game will be ruled on as shown:

A. **Super Classification.** Unlimited.

B. **Major Classification.** Twelve. The batter is ruled out for any in excess.

C. **Class A , Major Industrial and** Major Church **Classifications.** Six. The batter is ruled out for any in excess.

D. **Major Coed Classification.** Five. The batter is ruled out for any in excess.

NOTE: Both male and female home runs count toward the limit.

E. **Class B, Class A Industrial and all Masters and Seniors Classifications.** Three. The batter is ruled out for any in excess.

F. **Class A Coed Classification.** Two. The first batter hitting a home run in excess of two is ruled out and all other players hitting a home run are ruled out and disqualified from the game.

NOTE: Both male and female home runs count toward the limit.

G. **Class C and Class A Church Classifications.** One. The first batter hitting a home run in excess of one is ruled out and all other players hitting a home run are ruled out and disqualified from the game.

H. **Class D Classification.** None. The batter is ruled out for the first in excess and all other players hitting a home run are ruled out and disqualified from the game.

NOTE:

1. Any fair fly ball touched by a defensive player which then goes over the fence in fair territory, should be declared a four-base award and shall not be included in the total of over-the-fence home runs.

2. Any time the batter is ruled out because of the excessive home run rule, the ball is dead and no runners can advance.

3. A home run will be charged for any ball hit over the fence whether runs score or not.

4. A substitute can be entered for a disqualified player. If no substitutes are available, a team can play one player short. (See Rule 4, Section 1D)

SECTION 9. RUN AHEAD RULE (Code Article 209 F).

A. A run ahead rule must be used after five innings at all National Tournaments.

EXCEPTION: Men's Super Slow Pitch

1. Fast Pitch - Eight.
2. Modified Pitch - Ten.
3. Slow Pitch - Twelve.
4. Super Slow Pitch - 20 after four innings or 15 after five innings.

B. Complete innings must be played unless the home team scores the run ahead limit while at bat. Whenever a run ahead limit is used and the visiting team reaches the limit in the fifth or sixth inning, the home team must have their opportunity to bat in the bottom half of the inning.

SECTION 10. TIE-BREAKER (Code Article 209 H). (Women and Junior Olympic Girls Fast Pitch Only)

If, after the completion of nine innings of play, the score is tied, the following tie-breaker will be played to determine a winning team.

A. Starting with the top of the tenth inning, and each half inning thereafter, the offensive team shall begin its turn at bat with the player who is scheduled to bat ninth in that respective half inning being placed on second base. (e.g., if the number five batter is the lead off batter, the number four batter in the batting order will be placed on second base. A substitute may be inserted for the runner.) For scoring, see Rule 11, Section 10.

RULE 6 - PITCHING REGULATIONS (Fast Pitch)

SECTION 1. PRELIMINARIES.

Before starting the delivery (pitch), the pitcher shall comply with the following:

A. Both feet must be on the ground within the 24-inch length of the pitcher's plate. The shoulders shall be in line with first and third bases.

    1. **(Male Only)** He shall take a position with his pivot foot in contact with the pitcher's plate and his non-pivot foot on or behind the pitcher's plate.

    2. **(Female Only)** She shall take a position with both feet in contact with the pitcher's plate.

B. The pitcher shall take the signal from the catcher with the hands separated. The ball may be in the glove or pitching hand.

C. The pitcher shall hold the ball in both hands for not less than one second and not more than 10 seconds before releasing it.

    1. **(Male Only)** If the pitcher decides to pitch with the non-pivot foot to the rear and off the pitching plate, the backward step may be taken before, simultaneous with or after the hands are brought together. The pivot foot must remain in contact with the pitching plate at all times prior to the forward step.

    2. **(Female Only)** Both feet must remain in contact with the pitching plate at all times prior to the forward step.

D. The pitcher shall not be considered in pitching position unless the catcher is in position to receive the pitch.

E. The pitcher may not take the pitching position on or near the pitcher's plate without having the ball in his possession.

SECTION 2. STARTING THE PITCH.

The pitch starts when one hand is taken off the ball or the pitcher makes any motion that is part of his windup.

SECTION 3. LEGAL DELIVERY.

A. The pitcher must not make any motion to pitch without immediately delivering the ball to the batter.

B. The pitcher must not use a pitching motion in which, after having the ball in both hands in the pitching position, he removes one hand from the ball, takes a backward and forward swing, and returns the ball to both hands in front of the body.

C. The pitcher must not use a windup in which there is a stop or reversal of the forward motion.

D. The pitcher must not make two revolutions of the arm on the windmill pitch. A pitcher may drop his arm to the side and to the rear before starting the windmill motion.

E. The delivery must be an underhanded motion with the hand below the hip and the wrist not farther from the body than the elbow.

F. The release of the ball and follow through of the hand and wrist must be forward and past the straight line of the body.

G. In the act of delivering the ball, the pitcher must take one step simultaneous with the release of the ball. The step must be forward and toward the batter within the 24-inch length of the pitcher's plate.

NOTE: It is not a step if the pitcher slides his foot across the pitcher's plate, provided contact is maintained with the plate. Raising the foot off the pitching plate and returning it to the plate creates a rocking motion and is an illegal act.

H. Pushing off with the pivot foot from a place other than the pitcher's plate is illegal.

I. **(Female Only)** The pivot foot must remain in contact with or push off and drag away from the pitching plate prior to the front foot touching the ground, as long as the pivot foot remains in contact with the ground.

J. **(Male Only)** Both feet can be in the air at the same time. The leap is legal as long as the pivot foot does not replant and push off from a spot other than the pitching plate.

K. The pitcher must not continue to wind up after releasing the ball.

L. The pitcher shall not deliberately drop, roll or bounce the ball in order to prevent the batter from hitting it.

M. The pitcher has 20 seconds to release the next pitch after receiving the ball or after the umpire indicates "play ball."

SECTION 4. INTENTIONAL WALK.

If the pitcher desires to walk a batter intentionally all pitches must be legally delivered to the batter. A pitchout for the purpose of intentionally walking a batter is not considered an illegal pitch.

SECTION 5. DEFENSIVE POSITIONING.

A. The pitcher shall not deliver a pitch unless all defensive players are positioned in fair territory, except the catcher who must be in the catcher's box.

B. A fielder shall not take a position in the batter's line of vision or, with deliberate unsportsmanlike intent, acts in a manner to distract the batter. A pitch does not have to be released.

NOTE: The offending player shall also be ejected from the game.

C. The catcher or any other fielder shall not step on or in front of home plate without the ball, or touch the bat-

ter or his bat with a runner on third base trying to
score by means of a squeeze play or a steal.

NOTE: The batter shall also be awarded first base on
the obstruction and the ball is dead.

SECTION 6. FOREIGN SUBSTANCE.

The pitcher nor any other player shall not at any time
during the game be allowed to use any foreign substance
upon the ball. Under the supervision and control of the
umpire, powdered resin may be used to dry the hands.
The pitcher shall not wear tape on his fingers, a sweatband, bracelet, or similar type item on the wrist or forearm of the pitching arm.

EFFECT: An illegal pitch shall be called on the first offense.
If the pitcher continues to place a foreign substance on the
ball, he should be ejected from the ball game.

SECTION 7. CATCHER.

A. The catcher must remain within the lines of the
   catcher's box until the pitch is released.
B. The catcher shall return the ball directly to the pitcher
   after each pitch, except after a strikeout, a putout or
   an attempted putout made by the catcher.

   EXCEPTION: Does not apply with a runner(s) on
   base or the batter becoming a batter-runner.

SECTION 8. THROWING TO A BASE.

The pitcher shall not throw to a base during a live ball
while his foot is in contact with the pitcher's plate after
he has taken the pitching position. If the throw from the
pitcher's plate occurs during a live ball appeal play, the
appeal is canceled.

NOTE: The pitcher may remove himself from the pitching position by stepping backwards off the pitcher's
plate. Stepping forward or sideways constitutes an illegal
pitch.

EFFECT - Sections 1-8:
Any infraction of Sections 1-8 is an illegal pitch.

EFFECT:

A. The umpire shall give a delayed dead ball signal.

B. If the batter hits the ball and reaches first base safely, and if all other runners have advanced at least one base on the batted ball, the illegal pitch is cancelled. All action as a result of the batted ball stands. No option is given.

C. Otherwise the manager has the option to take the result of the play, or the illegal pitch is enforced by awarding a ball to the batter (if ball four award first base) and advancing all runners one base.

NOTE: If an illegal pitch hits the batter, the batter is awarded first base and all runners are awarded one base.

SECTION 9. WARM-UP PITCHES.

At the beginning of each half inning, or when a pitcher relieves another, not more than one minute may be used to deliver not more than five pitches. Play shall be suspended during this time. For excessive warm-up pitches, a pitcher shall be penalized by awarding a ball to the batter for each pitch in excess of five. This does not apply if the umpire delays the start of play due to substitution, conference, injuries, etc.

NOTE: A pitcher returning to pitch in the same half inning will not receive warm-up pitches.

NOTE: There is no limitation as to the number of times a player can return to the pitching position if he has not left the batting order or has not been removed from the pitcher's position by the umpire.

SECTION 10. NO PITCH.

No pitch shall be declared when:

A. The pitcher pitches during the suspension of play.

B. The pitcher attempts a quick return of the ball before the batter has taken his position or when the batter is off balance as a result of a previous pitch.

C. A runner is called out for leaving a base prior to the pitcher releasing the pitch.

D. The pitcher pitches before a runner has retouched his base after a foul ball has been declared and the ball is dead.

E. No player, manager or coach shall call time, employ any other word or phrase, or commit any act while the ball is alive and in play for the obvious purpose of trying to make the pitcher commit an illegal pitch. NOTE: A warning shall be issued to the offending team, and a repeat of this type act by any member of the team warned shall result in the offender being ejected from the game.

EFFECT - Section 10 A-E:

The ball is dead, and all subsequent action on that pitch is canceled.

SECTION 11. DROPPED BALL.

If the ball slips from the pitcher's hand during his delivery, a ball is declared on the batter, the ball will remain in play and the runners may advance at their own risk.

RULE 6 -
PITCHING REGULATIONS (Modified Pitch)

SECTION 1. PRELIMINARIES.

Before starting the delivery (pitch), the pitcher shall comply with the following:

A. He shall take a position with both feet in contact with the pitcher's plate. Both feet must be on the ground within the 24-inch length of the pitcher's. The shoulders shall be in line with first and third bases.

B. The pitcher shall take the signal from the catcher with the hands separated. The ball may be in the glove or pitching hand.

C. The pitcher shall hold the ball in both hands for not less than one second and not more than 10 seconds before releasing it.

D. The pitcher shall not be considered in pitching position unless the catcher is in position to receive the pitch.

E. The pitcher may not take the pitching position on or near the pitcher's plate without having the ball in his possession.

SECTION 2. STARTING THE PITCH.

The pitch starts when one hand is taken off the ball or the pitcher makes any motion that is part of his windup.

SECTION 3. LEGAL DELIVERY.

A. The pitcher must not make any motion to pitch without immediately delivering the ball to the batter.

B. The pitcher must not use a rocker action in which, after having the ball in both hands in the pitching position, he removes one hand from the ball, takes a backward and forward swing, and returns the ball to both hands in front of the body.

C. The pitcher must not use a windup in which there is a stop or reversal of the forward motion.

D. The pitcher may take the ball behind his back on the back swing.

E. The pitcher must not use a windmill or slingshot-type pitch or make a complete revolution in the delivery.

F. The ball must not be outside the pitcher's wrist on the downward motion and during the complete delivery.

G. The delivery must be underhanded motion with the hand below the hip and the pitcher's palm may be pointing downward.

H. On the forward swing of the pitching arm, the elbow must be locked at the point of release and the shoulders and driving hip must be squared to home plate when the ball is released.

I. The release of the ball must be on the first forward swing of the pitching arm past the hip. The release must have a complete, smooth follow-through with no abrupt stop of the arm near the hip.

J. In the act of delivering the ball, the pitcher must take one step simultaneous with the release of the ball. The step must be forward and toward the batter within the 24-inch length of the pitcher's plate.
NOTE: It is not a step if the pitcher slides his foot across the pitcher's plate, provided contact is maintained with the plate. Raising the foot off the pitching plate and returning it to the plate creates a rocking motion and is an illegal act.

K. Pushing off with the pivot foot from a place other than the pitcher's plate is illegal.

L. The pitcher must not continue to wind up after releasing the ball.

M. The pitcher shall not deliberately drop, roll or bounce the ball in order to prevent the batter from hitting it.

N. The pitcher has 20 seconds to release the next pitch after receiving the ball or after the umpire indicates "play ball".

SECTION 4. INTENTIONAL WALK.

If the pitcher desires to walk a batter intentionally all pitches must be legally delivered to the batter. A pitchout for the purpose of intentionally walking a batter is not considered an illegal pitch.

SECTION 5. DEFENSIVE POSITIONING.

A. The pitcher shall not deliver a pitch unless all defensive players are positioned in fair territory, except the catcher who must be in the catcher's box.

B. A fielder shall not take a position in the batter's line of vision or, with deliberate unsportsmanlike intent, acts in a manner to distract the batter. A pitch does not have to be released.
NOTE: The offending player shall also be ejected from the game.

C. The catcher or any other fielder shall not step on or in front of home plate without the ball, or touch the batter or his bat with a runner on third base trying to score by means of a squeeze play or a steal.
NOTE: The batter shall also be awarded first base on the obstruction and the ball is dead.

SECTION 6. FOREIGN SUBSTANCE.

The pitcher nor any other player shall not, at any time during the game, be allowed to use any foreign substance upon the ball. Under the supervision and control of the umpire, powdered resin may be used to dry the hands. The pitcher shall not wear tape on his fingers, a sweatband, bracelet, or similar type item on the wrist or forearm of the pitching arm.

SECTION 7. CATCHER.

A. The catcher must remain within the lines of the catcher's box until the pitch is released.

B. The catcher shall return the ball directly to the pitcher after each pitch, except after a strikeout, put out or an attempted put out made by the catcher.

EXCEPTION: Does not apply with a runner(s) on base or the batter becoming a batter-runner.

SECTION 8. THROWING TO A BASE.

The pitcher shall not throw to a base during a live ball while his foot is in contact with the pitcher's plate after he has taken the pitching position. If the throw from the pitcher's plate occurs during a live ball appeal play, the appeal is canceled.

NOTE: The pitcher may remove himself from the pitching position by stepping backwards off the pitcher's plate. Stepping forward or sideways constitutes an illegal pitch.

EFFECT - Sections 1-8:

Any infraction of Sections 1-8 is an illegal pitch.

EFFECT:

A. The umpire shall give a delayed dead ball signal.

B. If the batter hits the ball and reaches first base safely, and if all other runners have advanced at least one base on the batted ball, the illegal pitch is cancelled. All action as a result of the batted ball stands. No option is given.

C. Otherwise the manager has the option to take the result of the play, or the illegal pitch is enforced by awarding a ball to the batter (if ball four award first base) and advancing all runners one base.

NOTE: If an illegal pitch hits the batter, the batter is awarded first base and all runners are awarded one base.

SECTION 9. WARM-UP PITCHES.

At the beginning of each half inning, or when a pitcher relieves another, not more than one minute may be used to deliver not more than three pitches. Play shall be suspended during this time. For excessive warm-up pitches, a pitcher shall be penalized by awarding a ball to the batter for each pitch in excess of three.

NOTE: A pitcher returning to pitch in the same half inning will not receive warm-up pitches.

NOTE: There is no limitation as to the number of times a player can return to the pitching position if he has not left the batting order or has not been removed from the pitcher's position by the umpire.

SECTION 10. NO PITCH.

No pitch shall be declared when:

A. The pitcher pitches during the suspension of play.
B. The pitcher attempts a quick return of the ball before the batter has taken his position or when the batter is off balance as a result of a previous pitch.
C. A runner is called out for leaving a base prior to the pitcher releasing the pitch.
D. The pitcher pitches before a runner has retouched his base after a foul ball has been declared and the ball is dead.
E. No player, manager or coach shall call time, employ any other word or phrase, or commit any act while the ball is alive and in play for the obvious purpose of trying to make the pitcher commit an illegal pitch.
   NOTE: A warning shall be issued to the offending team, and a repeat of this type act by any member of the team warned shall result in the offender being ejected from the game.

EFFECT - Section 10 A-E:
   The ball is dead, and all subsequent action on that pitch is canceled.

SECTION 11. DROPPED BALL.

If the ball slips from the pitcher's hand during his delivery, a ball is declared on the batter, the ball will remain in play and the runners may advance at their own risk.

RULE 6 - PITCHING REGULATIONS (Slow Pitch)

SECTION 1. PRELIMINARIES.

A. The pitcher must take a position with both feet firmly on the ground and with one or both feet in contact with the pitcher's plate. The pitcher's pivot foot must be in contact with the pitcher's plate throughout the delivery.

B. The pitcher must come to a full and complete stop with the ball in front of the body. The front of the body must face the batter. This position must be maintained at least one second before starting the delivery.

C. The pitcher shall not be considered in pitching position unless the catcher is in position to receive the pitch.

SECTION 2. STARTING THE PITCH.

The pitch starts when the pitcher makes any motion that is part of his windup after the required stop. Prior to the required stop, any windup may be used.

SECTION 3. LEGAL DELIVERY.

A. The pitcher must not make any motion to pitch without immediately delivering the ball to the batter.

B. The windup is a continuous motion.

C. The pitcher must not use a windup in which there is a stop or reversal of the pitching motion.

D. The pitcher must deliver the ball toward home plate on the first forward swing of the pitching arm past the hip with an underhanded motion.

E. The pivot foot must remain in contact with the pitcher's plate until the pitched ball leaves the hand. If a step is taken, it can be forward, backward, or to the side, provided the pivot foot is in contact with the pitcher's plate and the step is simultaneous with the release of the ball.

F. The pitcher must not pitch the ball behind his back or through his legs.

G. The pitch shall be released at a moderate speed. The speed is left entirely up to the judgment of the umpire. The umpire shall warn the pitcher who delivers a pitch with excessive speed. If the pitcher repeats such an act after being warned, he shall be removed from the pitcher's position for the remainder of the game.

H. The ball must be delivered with perceptible arc and reach a height of at least six feet (1.83m) from the ground, while not exceeding a maximum height of 12 feet (3.66m) from the ground.

I. He does not continue to wind up after he releases the ball.

J. The pitcher has 10 seconds to release the next pitch after receiving the ball, or after the umpire indicates "play ball".

K. The pitcher shall not deliver a pitch from the glove.

SECTION 4. DEFENSIVE POSITIONING.

A. The pitcher shall not deliver a pitch unless all defensive players are positioned in fair territory, except the catcher who must be in the catcher's box..

B. A fielder shall not take a position in the batter's line of vision or, with deliberate unsportsmanlike intent, acts in a manner to distract the batter. A pitch does not have to be released.

NOTE: The offending player shall also be ejected from the game.

SECTION 5. FOREIGN SUBSTANCE.

The pitcher nor any other player shall not, at any time during the game, be allowed to use any foreign substance upon the ball, the pitching hand or the fingers. Under the supervision and control of the umpire, powdered resin may be used to dry the hands. The pitcher may wear a sweatband on the pitching arm or tape on the fingers.

SECTION 6. CATCHER.

A. The catcher must remain within the lines of the catcher's box until the pitched ball is batted, touches the ground or plate, or reaches the catcher's box.

B. The catcher shall return the ball directly to the pitcher after each pitch, except after a strikeout.
EFFECT: An additional ball is awarded to the batter.

SECTION 7. QUICK PITCH.

The pitcher shall not attempt a quick return of the ball before the batter has taken his position or when the batter is off balance as a result of a pitch.

EFFECT —Sections 1-7:

Any infraction of Sections 1-7 is an illegal pitch. A ball shall be called on the batter. Runners are not advanced.
EXCEPTION: If a batter swings at any illegal pitch, it is nullified and all play stands.

SECTION 8. WARM-UP PITCHES.

At the beginning of each half inning, or when a pitcher relieves another, not more than one minute may be used to deliver not more than three warm-up pitches. Play shall be suspended during this time. For excessive warm-up pitches, a pitcher shall be penalized by awarding a ball to the batter for each pitch.
NOTE: A pitcher returning to pitch in the same half inning will not receive warm-up pitches.

SECTION 9. NO PITCH.

No pitch shall be declared when:
A. The pitcher pitches during the suspension of play.

B. A runner is called out for leaving his base before the pitched ball reaches home plate, is batted, or touches the ground before home plate.

C. The pitcher pitches before a runner has retouched his base after a foul ball has been declared and the ball is dead.

D. The ball slips from the pitcher's hand during his windup or during the back swing.

E. No player, manager or coach shall call time, employ any other word or phrase, or commit any act while the ball is alive and in play for the obvious purpose of trying to make the pitcher commit an illegal pitch.
   NOTE: A warning shall be issued to the offending team, and a repeat of this type act by any member of the team warned shall result in the offender being removed from the game.

EFFECT: Section 9 A-E:
   The ball is dead, and all subsequent action on that pitch is canceled.

RULE 6 -
PITCHING REGULATIONS (16-Inch Slow Pitch)

SECTION 1. PRELIMINARIES.

A. The pitcher must take a position with both feet firmly on the ground and with one or both feet in contact with the pitcher's plate. The pitcher's pivot foot must be in contact with the pitcher's plate throughout the delivery.

B. The pitcher must come to a full and complete stop with the ball in front of the body. The front of the body must face the batter. This position must be maintained at least one second before starting the delivery.

C. The pitcher shall not be considered in pitching position unless the catcher is in position to receive the pitch.

D. While the pitcher is in the pitching position, in the motion for his delivery, or in the act of faking a delivery prior to a hesitation, the pivot foot must be in contact with the pitcher's plate. After a hesitation, the foot may leave the pitcher's plate during an attempted pickoff or a fake throw. When the pitching motion is restarted, the restriction takes effect again.

E. The pitcher may not take the pitching position on or near the pitcher's plate without having the ball in his possession.

SECTION 2. STARTING THE PITCH.

The pitch starts when the pitcher makes any motion that is part of his windup after the required stop. Prior to the required stop, any windup may be used.

SECTION 3. LEGAL DELIVERY.

A. The pivot foot must remain in contact with the

---

pitcher's plate until the pitched ball leaves the hand. If a step is taken, it can be forward, backward, or to the side, provided the pivot foot is in contact with the pitcher's plate and the step is simultaneous with the release of the ball.

B. The pitcher must not pitch the ball behind his back or through his legs.

C. The pitch shall be released at a moderate speed. The speed is left entirely up to the judgment of the umpire. The umpire shall warn the pitcher who delivers a pitch with excessive speed. If the pitcher repeats such an act after being warned, he shall be removed from the pitcher's position for the remainder of the game.

D. The ball must be delivered with a perceptible arc and reach a height of at least six feet (1.83m) from the ground, while not exceeding a maximum height of 12 feet (3.66m) from the ground

E. The pitcher must not continue to wind up after he releases the ball.

F. The pitcher must not commit a third hesitation before the mandatory delivery of a pitch, legal or illegal. Hesitations are defined as:

    1. Making any motion to pitch without immediately delivering the ball to the batter.

    2. Using a wind-up which is not a continuous motion.

    3. Using a wind-up in which there is a stop or reversal of the pitching motion.

    4. Not delivering the ball toward home plate on the first forward swing of the pitching arm past the hip.

NOTE:

    (a) After a hesitation of the pitching motion,

and before a restart of that motion, the pitcher may attempt or fake a throw for a pickoff with his pivot foot still in contact with the pitcher's plate.

(b) Runners may be off the bases without penalty during the delivery or fake delivery.

(c) During the pickoff attempt of the pitcher, or the catcher following a pitch, each runner must return to the base at which he was when the pitch was started, and before he is touched with the ball.

(d) If the ball is overthrown, no runners may advance.

(e) If the thrown ball remains in playable territory, the runners are in jeopardy until they return to their original bases.

G. The pitcher has 10 seconds to release the next pitch after receiving the ball, or after the umpire indicates "play ball."

SECTION 4. DEFENSIVE POSITIONING.

A. The pitcher shall not deliver a pitch unless all defensive players are positioned in fair territory, except the catcher who must be in the catcher's box.

B. A fielder shall not take a position in the batter's line of vision or, with deliberate unsportsmanlike intent, acts in a manner to distract the batter. A pitch does not have to be released.

NOTE: The offending player shall also be ejected from the game.

SECTION 5. FOREIGN SUBSTANCE.

The pitcher nor any other player shall not, at any time during the game, be allowed to use any foreign substance upon the ball, the pitching hand or the fingers. Under the supervision and control of the umpire, powdered resin may be used to dry the hands. The pitcher may wear a sweatband on the pitching arm or tape on the fingers.

SECTION 6. CATCHER.

A. The catcher must remain within the lines of the catcher's box until the pitched ball is batted, touches the ground or plate, or reaches the catcher's box.

B. The catcher shall return the ball directly to the pitcher after each pitch, except after a strikeout.
EFFECT: An additional ball is awarded to the batter.
EXCEPTION: Does not apply when the batter becomes a batter-runner or there are runners on base.

SECTION 7. QUICK PITCH.

The pitcher shall not attempt a quick return of the ball before the batter has taken his position or when the batter is off balance as a result of a pitch.

EFFECT —Sections 1-7: Any infraction of Sections 1-7 is an illegal pitch. A ball shall be called on the batter. Runners are not advanced.
EXCEPTION: If a batter swings at any illegal pitch, it is nullified and all play stands.

SECTION 8. WARM-UP PITCHES.

At the beginning of each half inning, or when a pitcher relieves another, not more than one minute may be used to deliver not more than three warm-up pitches. Play shall be suspended during this time. For excessive warm-up pitches, a pitcher shall be penalized by awarding a ball to the batter for each pitch.
NOTE: A pitcher returning to pitch in the same half inning will not receive warm-up pitches.

SECTION 9. NO PITCH.

No pitch shall be declared when:

A. The pitcher pitches during the suspension of play.

B. The pitcher pitches before a runner has retouched his base after a foul ball has been declared and the ball is dead.

C. The ball slips from the pitcher's hand during his windup or during the backswing.

D. No player, manager or coach shall call time, employ any other word or phrase, or commit any act while the ball is alive and in play for the obvious purpose of trying to make the pitcher commit an illegal pitch.
   NOTE: A warning shall be issued to the offending team, and a repeat of this type act by any member of the team warned shall result in the offender being removed from the game.

EFFECT - Section 9 A-E:

The ball is dead, and all subsequent action on that pitch is canceled.

RULE 7 - BATTING

SECTION 1. ON-DECK BATTER.

A. The on-deck batter is the offensive player whose name follows the name of the batter in the batting order.

B. The on-deck batter shall take a position within the lines of the on-deck circle nearest his bench.

C. The on-deck batter may loosen up with no more than two official softball bats, an approved warm-up bat, or a combination not to exceed two. Any detachable piece placed on the bat must be approved by the Equipment Standards Committee following a one-year period observed by members of this Committee.

D. The on-deck batter may leave the on-deck circle:

    1. When he becomes the batter.

    2. To direct runners advancing from third to home plate.

E. The on-deck batter may not interfere with the defensive player's opportunity to make an out

    1. If it involves a runner, the runner closest to home plate at the time of the interference shall be declared out.

    2. If it is with the defensive fielder fielding a fly ball, the batter is out.

SECTION 2. BATTING ORDER.

A. The batting order of each team showing the players' first and last name, uniform number and position must be on the lineup card and must be delivered before the game by the manager or captain to the plate umpire. The plate umpire shall submit it to the inspection of the manager or captain of the opposing team.

B. The batting order delivered to the umpire must be followed throughout the game, unless a player is replaced by a substitute. When this occurs, the substitute must take the place of the removed player in the batting order.

C. The first batter in each inning shall be the batter whose name follows that of the last player who completed his turn at bat in the preceding inning.

EFFECT - Section 2 B-C:

Except for a wrong batter at bat, batting out of order is an appeal play which may be made only by the defensive team. The defensive team forfeits its right to appeal batting out of order when one legal or illegal pitch has been made to the following batter, or when the pitcher and all infielders have clearly vacated their normal fielding positions and have left fair territory on their way to the bench or dugout.

   1. If the error is discovered while the incorrect batter is at bat, the correct batter may take his place and legally assume any balls and strikes. Any runs scored or bases run while the incorrect batter was at bat shall be legal.
   NOTE: The offensive team may correct a wrong batter at the plate with no penalty.

   2. If the error is discovered after the incorrect batter has completed his turn at bat and before a legal or illegal pitch has been made to the following batter or before the pitcher and all infielders have clearly vacated their normal fielding positions and have left fair territory on their way to the bench or dugout area: (a) the player who should have batted is out. (b) Any advance or score made because of a ball batted by the improper batter or because of the improper batter's advance to first base as a result of obstruction, and error, a hit batter, walk, dropped third strike or a base hit shall be

nullified. (c) The next batter is the player whose
name follows that of the player called out for
failing to bat. (d) If the batter declared out
under these circumstances is the third out, the
correct batter in the next inning shall be the
player who would have come to bat had the
player been put out by ordinary play.
3. If the error is discovered after the first legal or
illegal pitch to the next batter, or after the
pitcher and all infielders have clearly vacated
their normal fielding positions and have left fair
territory on their way to the bench or dugout
area, the turn at bat of the incorrect batter is
legal, all runs scored and bases run are legal and
the next batter in order shall be the one whose
name follows that of the incorrect batter. No
one is called out for failure to bat. Players who
have not batted and who have not been called
out have lost their turn at bat until reached
again in the regular order.
4. No runner shall be removed from the base he is
occupying except the batter-runner who has
been taken off the base by the umpire as in (2)
above to bat in his proper place. He merely
misses his turn at bat with no penalty. The batter following him in the batting order becomes
the legal batter.
D. The batting order for coed shall alternate the sexes.
Coed play will use an 11-inch red-stitch ball when the
female bats and an 12-inch red stitch ball when the
male bats.
E. When the third out in an inning is made before the
batter has completed his turn at bat, he shall be the
first batter in the next inning and the ball and strike
count on him shall be canceled.

SECTION 3. BATTING POSITION.

A. The batter must have both feet completely within the
   lines of the batter's box prior to the start of the pitch.
   He may touch the lines, but no part of a foot may be
   outside the lines prior to the pitch.

B. The batter must take his position within 10 seconds
   after "play ball" has been declared by the umpire.
   EFFECT: The umpire will call a strike. No pitch has
   to be thrown and the ball remains dead.

C. The batter shall not step directly in front of the
   catcher to the other batter's box while the pitcher is in
   position to pitch.
   EFFECT: The ball is dead, the batter is out and the
   runners may not advance.

SECTION 4. A STRIKE IS CALLED BY THE UMPIRE.

A. (Fast Pitch Only) For each legally pitched ball enter-
   ing the strike zone.
   EFFECT: The ball is in play and the runners may
   advance with liability to be put out.
   (Slow Pitch Only) For each legally pitched ball enter-
   ing the strike zone before touching the ground and
   the batter does not swing. It is not a strike if the
   pitched ball touches home plate and then is swung at
   by the batter. Any pitched ball that hits the ground or
   plate cannot be legally swung at by the batter.
   NOTE: If the batter swings and misses the pitch prior
   to the ball hitting the ground or plate, it is a strike.
   EFFECT: The ball is dead.

B. For each legally pitched ball struck at and missed by
   the batter.
   FAST PITCH EFFECT: The ball is in play and the
   runners may advance with liability to be put out.
   SLOW PITCH EFFECT: The ball is dead. If the batter
   swings at an illegal pitch, the illegal pitch is nullified.

C. For each foul tip.
   EFFECT: (Fast Pitch Only) The ball is in play and runners may advance with liability to be put out. The batter is out if it is the third strike.
   (Slow Pitch Only) The ball is dead and the batter is out if it is the third strike.
   (16-Inch Slow Pitch) The ball remains live; runners cannot advance.

D. (Fast Pitch Only) For each foul ball when the batter has fewer than two strikes.

E. (Slow Pitch Only) For each foul ball, including the third strike.
   NOTE: A caught ball is not a foul ball.

F. For each pitched ball struck at and missed which touches any part of the batter.

G. When any part of the batter's person or clothing is hit with his own batted ball when he is in the batter's box and has fewer than two strikes.

H. When a delivered ball by the pitcher hits the batter while the ball is in the strike zone.

I. If the batter does not take his position within 10 seconds after "play ball" has been declared.

EFFECT - Section 4 D-I:
   The ball is dead and each runner must return to his base without liability to be put out.

SECTION 5. A BALL IS CALLED BY THE UMPIRE.

A. (Fast Pitch Only) For each legally pitched ball which does not enter the strike zone, or touches the ground before reaching home plate, or touches home plate and the batter does not swing.
   EFFECT: The ball is in play and runners are entitled to advance with liability to be put out.
   (Slow Pitch Only) For each legally pitched ball which does not enter the strike zone, touches the ground

before reaching home plate, or touches home plate, and the batter does not swing. Any pitched ball that hits the ground or plate cannot be legally swung at by the batter.

NOTE: If the batter swings at a pitch after the ball hits the ground or plate, it is a ball.

EFFECT: The ball is dead and runners may not advance.

(16-Inch Slow Pitch): The ball remains live; however, runners cannot advance.

B. (Fast Pitch Only) For each illegally pitched ball not swung at.

EFFECT: The ball is dead and runners are entitled to advance one base without liability to be put out.

(Slow Pitch Only) For each illegally pitched ball not swung at.

EFFECT: The ball is dead and runners may not advance.

C. (Slow Pitch Only) When a pitched ball hits the batter outside the strike zone.

D. When the catcher fails to return the ball directly to the pitcher as required.

E. For each excessive warm-up pitch.

EFFECT - Section 5 C-E:

The ball is dead and runners may not advance.

SECTION 6. THE BATTER IS OUT.

A. When the third strike is struck at, missed and the pitched ball touches any part of the batter's person.

B. When a batter enters the batter's box with or is discovered using an altered bat. The batter is also ejected from the game.

C. When the batter enters the batter's box with or is discovered using an illegal bat.

D. When an entire foot is touching the ground com-

      pletely outside the lines of the batter's box when he
      hits a ball fair or foul.

E. When any part of a foot is touching home plate when
    he hits a ball fair or foul.

F. (Fast Pitch Only) When the batter bunts foul after the
    second strike. If the ball is caught in the air, it remains
    live and in play.

G. (Slow Pitch Only) When the batter bunts or chops
    the ball.

H. When members of the team at bat interfere with a
    player attempting to field a fly ball.

I. When the batter hits a fair ball with the bat a second
    time in fair territory.
    EXCEPTION: If the batter is standing in the batter's
    box and contact is made while the bat is in the batter's
    hands, a foul ball is ruled even if the ball is hit a sec-
    ond time over fair territory.
    NOTE: If the batter drops the bat and the ball rolls
    against the bat in fair territory, and, in the umpires
    judgment, there was no intention to interfere with the
    course of the ball, the batter is not out and the ball is
    live and in play.
    EFFECT - Section 6 A-I: The ball is dead and each
    runner must return to the base legally held at the time
    of the pitch.

J. (Slow Pitch Only) After a third strike, including a
    foul ball that is hit after two strikes.
    EXCEPTION: If a fly ball is caught, the ball remains
    live.

K. When a called or swinging third strike is caught by
    the catcher.

L. (Fast Pitch Only) When the batter has three strikes
    if there are fewer than two outs and first base is
    occupied.

> NOTE: If the batter runs toward first base and draws a throw to first base in violation of the 'third strike rule,' the umpire shall declare a dead ball and all runners must return to the last base occupied at the time of the pitch.
> EXCEPTION: (Junior Olympic 10-Under)

M. Whenever the exception under Rule 4, Section 1D (Short-handed Rule) applies.

N. The batter shall not hinder the catcher from catching or throwing the ball by stepping out of the batter's box, or intentionally hinder the catcher while standing within the batter's box.

EFFECT: The ball is dead, the batter is out and each runner must return to the last base that, in the judgment of the umpire, was touched at the time of the interference.

RULE 8 - BATTER-RUNNER AND RUNNER

SECTION 1.

THE BATTER BECOMES A BATTER-RUNNER.

A. As soon as he legally hits a fair ball.

B. (Fast Pitch Only) When the catcher fails to catch the third strike before the ball touches the ground when there are fewer than two outs and first base is unoccupied, or anytime there are two outs. This is called the third strike rule. (See NOTE in Rule 7-6 L.)

   EXCEPTION: (Junior Olympic 10-Under) The ball is dead and the batter is out.

EFFECT - Section 1 A-B:

   The ball is in play, and the batter becomes a batter-runner with liability to be put out.

C. When four balls have been called by the umpire. The batter-runner is awarded one base without liability to be put out.

   EFFECT:

   1. (Fast Pitch Only) The ball is in play unless it has been blocked.

   2. (Slow Pitch Only) The ball is dead and runners may not advance unless forced. If the pitcher desires to walk a batter intentionally, he may do so by notifying the plate umpire who shall award the batter first base. If two batters are to be walked intentionally, the second intentional walk may not be administered until the first batter reaches first base.
   NOTE: If the umpire mistakenly allows two walks at one time and the first batter fails to touch first base, no appeal will be honored on the first batter.

   3. (Coed) The ball is dead. On any walk to a male

batter (intentional or not), the next batter - a
female - has her choice of walking or hitting up
until the first pitch.

NOTE: Should the female batter-runner pass a
male batter-runner when choosing to walk, no
out shall be called during this dead ball period.
A male batter-runner advancing to second without touching first base shall be called out if
properly appealed.

D. When the catcher obstructs, hinders or prevents the
batter from striking or hitting a pitched ball.
EFFECT:

  1. The umpire shall give a delayed dead ball signal.
  2. If the batter hits the ball and reaches first base
     safely, and if all other runners have advanced at
     least one base on the batted ball, catcher
     obstruction is canceled. All action as a result of
     the batted ball stands. No option is given.

     NOTE: Once a runner has passed a base, he is
     considered to have reached that base (whether
     missing the base or not) and no option is given.

  3. If the manager does not take the result of the
     play, obstruction is enforced by awarding the
     batter first base and advancing all other runners
     only if forced.

E. When a fair batted ball strikes the person, attached
equipment, or clothing of an umpire or a runner. If
the runner is hit with a fair batted ball while touching
a base, he is not out.
EFFECT:

  1. If, after touching a fielder (including the
     pitcher), the ball is in play.
  2. If, after passing a fielder other than the pitcher,
     and no other infielder had a chance to make an

out, the ball is in play.

3. If before passing a fielder without being touched, the ball is dead. If the runner is hit by the ball while off base, he is out and the batter-runner is entitled to first base without liability to be put out. Any runner not forced by the batter-runner must return to the base he had reached prior to the interference. When a fair ball touches a runner who is in contact with a base, the ball remains dead or live depending on the position of the fielder closest to the base.

F. (Fast Pitch Only) When a pitched ball not swung at nor called a strike touches any part of the batter's person or clothing while he is in the batter's box. It does not matter if the ball strikes the ground before hitting him. The batter's hands are not to be considered a part of the bat.

EFFECT: The ball is dead. The batter is entitled to one base without liability to be put out.

EXCEPTION: If no attempt is made to avoid being hit, the umpire calls either a ball or a strike.

SECTION 2. BATTER-RUNNER IS OUT.

A. (Fast Pitch Only) When the catcher drops the third strike and he is legally put out prior to reaching first base.

B. When after hitting a fair ball he is legally put out prior to reaching first base.

C. When, after a fly ball is hit, the ball is caught by a fielder before it touches the ground, any object or person other than a defensive player.

EFFECT - Section 2 A-C:

The ball is in play.

D. When he fails to advance to first base and enters his team area after a batted fair ball, a base on balls, a hits batsman (Fast Pitch Only), a dropped third strike (Fast Pitch Only), or catcher obstruction.

EXCEPTION: In slow pitch, the ball is dead on a base on balls, the batter-runner is out and runners cannot advance.

E. When he runs outside the three-foot (0.91m) lane and, in the judgment of the umpire, interferes with the fielder taking the throw at first base; however, he may run outside the three-foot (0.91m) lane to avoid a fielder attempting to field a batted ball.

F. When he interferes with a fielder attempting to field a batted ball, interferes with a fielder attempting to throw the ball, intentionally interferes with a thrown ball, makes contact with a fair batted ball before reaching first base, or (Fast Pitch Only) interferes with a dropped third strike. If this interference, in the judgment of the umpire, is an obvious attempt to prevent a double play, the runner closest to home plate shall also be called out.

NOTE: A batter-runner being hit with a thrown ball does not necessarily constitute interference.

G. When he interferes with a play at home plate in an attempt to prevent an obvious out at home plate. The runner is also out.

H. When he moves back toward home plate to avoid or delay a tag by a fielder.

EFFECT - Section 2 E-H:

The ball is dead and runner(s) must return to the last base legally touched at the time of interference.

I. When he hits an infield fly.

J. When an infielder intentionally drops a fair fly ball, including a line drive or a bunt, which can be caught with ordinary effort with first; first and second; first and third; or first, second and third bases occupied

---

with fewer than two outs. A trapped ball shall not be considered as having been intentionally dropped.

EFFECT: The ball is dead, and each runner must return to the last base touched at the time of the pitch.

NOTE: If an infield fly is ruled, it has precedence over an intentionally dropped ball.

K. When the immediate preceding runner who is not yet out intentionally interferes, in the umpire's judgment, with a fielder who is attempting to catch a thrown ball or throw a ball in an attempt to complete the play.

EFFECT: Batter-runner is out. The runner shall also be called out.

L. (Slow Pitch Only) For excess over-the-fence home runs.

SECTION 3. TOUCHING BASES IN LEGAL ORDER.

A. When a runner must return to a base while the ball is in play or dead, he must touch the base(s) in reverse order.

EXCEPTION: Should time out be called while a runner is touching a base, he must remain on the base occupied.

B. When a runner or batter-runner acquires the right to a base by touching it before being put out, he is entitled to hold the base until he has legally touched the next base in order or is forced to vacate it for a succeeding runner.

C. When a runner dislodges a base from its proper position, neither he nor the succeeding runner(s) in the same series of plays are compelled to follow a base out of position.

EFFECT - Section 3 B-C:

The ball is in play and runners may advance or return with liability to be put out.

D. A runner shall not run bases in reverse order either to confuse the fielders or to make a travesty of the game.
EFFECT: The ball is dead and the runner is out.

E. Two runners may not occupy the same base simultaneously.
EFFECT: The runner who first legally occupied the base shall be entitled to it, unless forced to advance. The other runner may be put out by being touched with the ball.

F. Failure of a PRECEDING runner to touch a base or to legally tag up on a caught fly ball, and who is declared out, does not affect the status of a SUCCEEDING runner who touches bases in proper order. If the failure to touch a base in regular order or to legally tag up on a caught fly ball is the third out of the inning, no SUCCEEDING runner may score a run.

G. No runner may return to touch a missed base or one he had left too soon after a following runner has scored or once he leaves the field of play.

H. Bases left too soon on a caught fly ball must be retouched prior to advancing to awarded bases.

I. Awarded bases must be touched in legal order.

SECTION 4. RUNNERS ARE ENTITLED TO ADVANCE WITH LIABILITY TO BE PUT OUT.

A. (Fast Pitch Only) When the ball leaves the pitcher's hand on his delivery.

B. On a thrown ball or a fair batted ball that is not blocked.

C. On a thrown ball that hits an umpire.

D. When a legally caught fly ball is first touched.

E. If a fair ball strikes an umpire or a runner after having passed an infielder other than the pitcher, and provided no other infielder had a chance to make an out, or when a fair batted ball has been touched by an infielder, including the pitcher.

EFFECT - Section 4 A-E:

The ball is in play.

SECTION 5. A RUNNER FORFEITS HIS EXEMPTION FROM LIABILITY TO BE PUT OUT.

A. If, while the ball is in play or on awarded bases, he fails to touch a base before attempting to make the next base. If the runner put out is the batter-runner at first base, or any other runner forced to advance because the batter became a batter-runner, this is a force out.

B. If, after overrunning first base, the runner attempts to continue to second base.

C. If, after dislodging a base, a runner attempts to continue to the next base.

D. (16-Inch Slow Pitch Only) A runner may lead off any base with the risk of being picked off by a throw from the pitcher or catcher. If a throw results in an overthrown or blocked ball, no runners may advance. Any runner advancing on a pitch not hit is liable to be put out if tagged before returning to his original base.

SECTION 6. RUNNERS ARE ENTITLED TO ADVANCE WITHOUT LIABILITY TO BE PUT OUT.

A. When forced to vacate a base because the batter was awarded a base on balls.

EFFECT: (Fast Pitch Only) The ball remains in play unless it is blocked. Any runner affected is entitled to one base and may advance farther at his own risk if the ball is in play. (Slow Pitch Only) The ball is dead.

B. When a fielder not in possession of the ball, not in the act of fielding a batted ball, or not about to receive a thrown ball, impedes the progress of a runner or batter-runner who is legally running bases.

NOTE: Obstructed runners are still required to touch all bases in proper order, or they could be called out on a proper appeal by the defensive team.

1. If the obstructed runner is put out prior to reaching the base he would have reached had there not been obstruction, a dead ball is called and the obstructed runner and each other runner affected by the obstruction will always be awarded the base or bases he would have reached, in the umpire's judgment, had there not been obstruction. An obstructed runner may never be called out between the two bases where he was obstructed. This runner would either be advanced or returned to the last base touched. Should an act of interference occur following any obstruction, enforcement of the interference penalty would have precedence.

2. If the obstructed runner is put out after passing the base he would have reached had there not been obstruction, the obstructed runner will be called out. The ball remains live.

3. When a runner, while advancing or returning to a base, is obstructed by a fielder who neither has the ball nor is attempting to field a batted or thrown ball, or a fielder who fakes a tag without the ball, the obstructed runner and each other runner affected by the obstruction, will always be awarded the base or bases he would have reached, in the umpire's judgment, had there been no obstruction. If the umpire feels there is justification, a defensive player making a fake tag could be ejected from the game.

4. Catcher obstruction on the batter is covered under Rule 8, Section 1D.
   EFFECT: When any obstruction occurs (including a rundown), the umpire will signal a delayed dead ball. The ball will remain alive.

C. (Fast Pitch Only) When a wild pitch or passed ball lodges in or goes under, over or through the backstop.
   EFFECT: The ball is dead and all runners are awarded one base only. The batter is awarded first base only on the fourth ball.

D. When forced to vacate a base because the batter was awarded first base.

E. (Fast Pitch Only) When a pitcher makes an illegal pitch, providing the offensive coach does not take the result of the play.

F. When a fielder intentionally contacts or catches a fair batted or thrown ball with his cap, helmet, mask, protector, pocket, detached glove or any part of his uniform which is detached from its proper place on his person.
   EFFECT: The runners would be entitled to three bases from the time of the pitch if a batted ball, or two bases from the time of the throw if a thrown ball, and in either case, they may advance farther at their own risk. If the illegal catch or touch is made on a fair hit ball which, in the judgment of the umpire, would have cleared the outfield fence in flight, the batter-runner shall be awarded a four base award.

G. When the ball is in play and is overthrown (beyond the boundary lines) or is blocked.
   EFFECT: All runners will be awarded two bases, and the award will be governed by the positions of the runners when the ball left the fielder's hand. If two runners are between the same bases, the award is based on the position of the lead runner.

EXCEPTION:
   1. When a fielder loses possession of the ball, such as on an attempted tag, and the ball enters the dead ball area or becomes blocked, each runner is awarded one base from the last base touched at the time the ball entered the dead ball area or became blocked.
   2. If a runner touches the next base and returns to his original base, the original base he left is considered the last base touched for the purpose of an overthrow award.
   3. If the ball becomes blocked due to offensive equipment not involved in the game, the ball is ruled dead and runners are returned to the last base touched at the time of the blocked ball. If the blocked ball prevented the defense from making a play, the runner being played on is called out. (If this player has scored prior to the blocked ball being ruled, the runner closest to home is called out.)
H. When a fair batted fly ball strikes the foul pole above the fence level or leaves the playing field in fair territory without touching the ground or going through the fence. It shall entitle the batter-runner to a home run, unless it passes out of the grounds at a distance less than the prescribed fence distances from home plate, in which case the batter-runner would be entitled to only two bases.
I. When a fair ball bounces over or rolls under or through a fence or any designated boundary of the playing field. Also, when it deflects off of a defensive player and goes out of play in foul territory, deflects off a runner or umpire after having passed an infielder excluding the pitcher and provided no other infielder

had a chance to make an out.

EFFECT: The ball is dead, and all runners are awarded two bases from the time of the pitch.

J. When a live ball is unintentionally carried by a fielder from playable territory into dead ball territory.

EFFECT: The ball is dead and each runner is awarded one base from the last base touched at the time the fielder entered dead ball territory.

NOTE: A fielder carrying a live ball into the dugout or team area to tag a player is considered to have unintentionally carried it there.

K. If, in the judgment of the umpire, a fielder intentionally carries, kicks, pushes or throws a live ball from playable territory into dead ball territory.

EFFECT: The ball is dead. Each runner is awarded two bases from the last base touched at the time the fielder entered or the ball was kicked, pushed or thrown into dead ball territory.

SECTION 7.
A RUNNER MUST RETURN TO HIS BASE.

A. When a batted ball is foul.

B. When an illegally batted ball is declared by the umpire.

C. When a batter, batter-runner or runner is called out for interference. Each other runner shall return to the last base which, in the umpire's judgment, was legally touched by him at the time of the interference.

D. (Fast Pitch Only) When any part of the batter's person or clothing is touched by a pitched ball that is swung at and missed.

E. (Fast Pitch Only) When a batter is hit by a pitched ball, unless forced.

EFFECT - Section 7 A-E:

    1. The ball is dead.

2. Each runner must return to his base without liability to be put out, except when forced to go to the next base because the batter became a batter-runner.

3. Runners need not touch the intervening bases in returning to base.

F. (Fast Pitch Only) When the plate umpire or his clothing interferes with the catcher's attempt to throw out a runner stealing.

EXCEPTION: If the runner being played on is ruled out, he will remain out.

G. (Slow Pitch Only) Base stealing is not allowed.

EFFECT: Each runner may leave his base when a pitched ball is batted, touches the ground or reaches home, but must return to that base immediately after each pitch not hit by the batter.

EXCEPTION: (16-Inch Slow Pitch Only) Runners may lead off prior to a pitched ball.

H. When an intentionally dropped ball is ruled.

I. (Fast Pitch Junior Olympic 10-Under Only) Under no condition is a runner permitted to steal a base when a pitched ball is not batted. Each runner may leave his base when the ball leaves the pitcher's hand, but the ball is dead if not hit, and he must return to his base without liability to be put out.

SECTION 8. THE RUNNER IS OUT.

A. When running to any base in regular or reverse order and he runs more than three feet (0.91 m) from a direct line between that base and the next one to avoid being touched by the ball in the hand(s) of a fielder.

B. When the ball is in play and while he is not in contact with a base, he is legally touched with the ball in the hand(s) of a fielder.

C. When, on a force play, a fielder contacts the base while holding the ball, touches the ball to the base or tags the runner before he reaches the base.

D. When he fails to return to touch the base he previously occupied or missed and is properly appealed.

E. When he physically passes a preceding runner before that runner has been put out.

EFFECT - Section 8 A-E:

The ball is in play and the runner is out.

F. When he leaves his base to advance to another base before a caught fly ball has touched a fielder, provided the ball is returned to an infielder and properly appealed.

G. When he fails to touch the intervening base or bases in regular or reverse order and the ball is returned to an infielder and properly appealed.

H. When the batter-runner legally overruns first base, attempts to run to second base and is legally touched while off base.

I. When running or sliding for home plate and he fails to touch it, makes no attempt to return to it, and a fielder properly appeals while touching the plate and appeals to the umpire for the decision.

EFFECT Section 8 F-I:

1. These are appeal plays, and the defensive team loses the privilege of putting the runner out if: (a) the appeal is not made before the next legal or illegal pitch, (b) before the pitcher and all infielders have clearly vacated their normal fielding positions and have left fair territory on their way to the bench or dugout area, or (c) on the last play of the game, the appeal can be made until the umpires leave the field of play.

2. (Live Ball Appeal) If properly appealed during a

live ball, the runner is out. (POE # 1 B)
3. (Dead Ball Appeal) Once the ball has been returned to the infield and time has been called, any infielder (including the pitcher or catcher), with or without possession of the ball, may make a verbal appeal on a runner missing a base or leaving a base too soon on a caught fly ball. The administering umpire should acknowledge the appeal and then make a decision on the play. No runner may leave his base during this period as the ball remains dead until the next pitch.

NOTE:

(a) If the ball goes out of play, the dead ball appeal cannot be made until the umpire places a new ball into the game.

(b) If the pitcher has possession of the ball and is in contact with the pitching plate when making a verbal appeal, no illegal pitch is called.

(c) If "play ball" has been declared by the umpire and the pitcher then requests an appeal, the umpire would again call "time" and allow the appeal process.

J. When he interferes with a fielder attempting to field a batted ball, interferes with a fielder attempting to throw the ball or intentionally interferes with a thrown ball. If this interference, in the judgment of the umpire, is an obvious attempt to prevent a double play and occurs before the runner is put out, the immediate succeeding runner shall also be called out.

NOTE: If a ball ricochets off one defensive player and another player has the opportunity to make an out, the runner will be ruled out if he interferes with the second fielder.

K. When he is struck with a fair untouched batted ball while not in contact with a base and before it passes an infielder, excluding the pitcher.

NOTE - Section 8 J-K:

When runners are called out for interference, the batter-runner is awarded first base and credited with a base hit.

L. When he intentionally kicks a ball which an infielder has missed.

M. When anyone, other than another runner, physically assists him while the ball is in play. If this assistance occurs prior to a caught batted fly ball, regardless of whether the ball is fair or foul, a delayed dead ball call will be made, after which he will be declared out. If the ball is caught, the batter-runner will also be declared out.

EFFECT: The ball is dead if not caught. If a fair ball, award the batter-runner one base and if a foul ball, the batter will bat again. This includes a home run.

N. When the coach near third base runs in the direction of home plate on or near the baseline while a fielder is attempting to make a play on a batted or thrown ball and thereby draws a throw to home plate. The runner closest to home shall be declared out.

O. When one or more members of the offensive team stand or collect around a base to which a runner is advancing, thereby confusing the fielders and adding to the difficulty of making the play.

NOTE: Members of a team include bat boy or any other person authorized to sit on the team's bench.

P. When a coach intentionally interferes with a thrown ball while in the coach's box, or interferes with the defensive team's opportunity to make a play on another runner. The runner closest to home plate at the time of the interference shall be declared out.

EFFECT - Section 8 J-P: The ball is dead and the runner is out. Each other runner must return to the last base legally touched at the time of the interference.

Q. When, after being declared out or after scoring, a runner interferes with a defensive player's opportunity to make a play on another runner.

EFFECT: The runner closest to home plate at the time of the interference shall be declared out.

R. When a defensive player has the ball and the runner remains on his feet and deliberately, with great force, crashes into the defensive player.

EFFECT: The runner is out, the ball is dead, and each other runner must return to the last base touched at the time of the interference.

NOTE: If the act is determined to be flagrant, the offender shall be ejected.

S. (Slow Pitch Only) When he fails to keep contact with the base to which he is entitled until a pitched ball touches the ground, reaches home plate or is batted.

EXCEPTION: (16-Inch Slow Pitch Only) Any runner may leave his base as soon as the ball is declared in play.

T. (Fast Pitch Only) When he fails to keep contact with the base to which he is entitled until the ball leaves the pitcher's hand.

EFFECT: Section S-T:

The ball is dead, "no pitch" is declared and the runner is out.

U. (Fast Pitch Only) When a runner is legitimately off his base after a pitch or as a result of a batter completing his turn at bat, and while the pitcher has the ball within an eight foot (2.44m) radius of the pitcher's plate, he must immediately return to his base or attempt to advance to the next base.

1. Failure to immediately return to his base or proceed to the next base once the pitcher has the ball within the eight foot (2.44 m) radius of the pitcher's plate will result in the runner being declared out.

2. Once the runner returns to a base for any reason, he will be declared out if he leaves the base, unless a play is made on him or another runner (a fake throw is considered a play), the pitcher no longer has possession of the ball within the eight foot (2.44 m) radius, or the pitcher releases the ball on a pitch to the batter.

   NOTE: A base on balls or dropped third strike on which any runner is entitled to run past any base is treated the same as a batted ball. The batter-runner may continue past any base and is entitled to run as long as he does not stop. If he stops after he rounds any base, he then must comply with (1) above.

V. When he abandons a base and enters his team area or leaves the field of play.

W. When he positions himself behind and not in contact with a base to get a running start on any fly ball. The ball remains alive.

X. (Slow Pitch Only Except Coed) Whenever the exception under Rule 4, Section 1D applies.

SECTION 9. RUNNER IS NOT OUT.

A. When he runs behind or in front of the fielder and outside the baseline in order to avoid interfering with a fielder attempting to field the ball in the base path.

B. When he does not run in a direct line to a base, provided the fielder in the direct line does not have the ball in his possession.

C. When more than one fielder attempts to field a batted ball and the runner comes into contact with the one who, in the judgment of the umpire, could not have made an out.

D. When he is hit with a fair, untouched batted ball that has passed an infielder, excluding the pitcher, and, in the judgment of the umpire, no other infielder had a chance to make an out.

E. When he is hit with a fair untouched batted ball over foul territory that, in the judgement of the umpire, no infielder had a chance to make an out.

F. When he is hit by a fair batted ball after it touches, or is touched by, any fielder, including the pitcher, and he could not avoid contact with the ball.

G. When he is touched with a ball not securely held by a fielder.

H. When the defensive team does not request the umpire's decision on an appeal play until after the next legal or illegal pitch, or until after the pitcher and all infielders have clearly vacated their normal fielding positions and have left fair territory on their way to the bench or dugout area.

I. When a batter-runner overruns first base after touching it and returns directly to the base.

J. When he is not given sufficient time to return to a base. He will not be called out for being off base before the pitcher releases the ball. "No pitch" will be called by the umpire.

K. When he has legally started to advance. He may not be stopped by the pitcher receiving the ball while on the pitching plate, nor by the pitcher stepping on the plate with the ball in his possession.

L. When he holds his base until a fly ball touches a

fielder and then attempts to advance.

M. When hit by a batted ball when touching his base, unless he inten-tionally interferes with the ball or a fielder making a play. (See Rule 8, Section 1 E (1-3).)

N. When he slides into a base and dislodges it from its proper position. The base is considered to have followed the runner.

EFFECT: A runner reaching a base safely will not be out for being off that base if it becomes dislodged. He may return without liability to be put out when the base has been replaced. A runner forfeits this exemption if he attempts to advance beyond the dislodged base before it is again in proper position.

O. When a fielder makes a play on a batter, batter-runner or runner while using an illegal glove. The manager of the offended team is given two options:

1. He may have the entire play nullified with each runner returning to his original base and the batter batting over again, assuming the ball and strike count he had prior to the pitch he hit.

2. He may take the result of the play and disregard the illegal act.

SECTION 10. RUNNING (Senior Men's Only).

A. A courtesy runner shall be allowed once per inning for any reason. The courtesy runner must be the last recorded out (or the player scheduled to bat last, if in the first inning with no outs) and must be entered prior to the first pitch to the next batter. The courtesy runner is officially in the game when "play ball" has been declared by the umpire. An ineligible courtesy runner is an appeal situation that must be made before a legal or illegal pitch to the next batter.

EFFECT: The use of an ineligible courtesy runner shall result in the removal of the runner from the base and an out being recorded on the player whom he replaced.

B. Runners must touch the second home plate located adjacent to the right handed batter's box in order to be safe at home. Defensive players can only touch the original home plate and runners can only touch the second home plate. Runners tagged by the defensive team will not be out. If the runner touches the original home plate, he will be out and the ball will remain live. (See diagram under Rule 2, Section 3G)

C. Once a runner crosses a line 20 feet from home plate, he cannot return to third base.

EFFECT: The runner will be called out if he returns and the ball remains live.

RULE 9 - PROTESTS

SECTION 1. Protests will not be received or considered if they are based solely on a decision involving the accuracy of judgment on the part of an umpire. Examples of protests which will not be considered are:

A. Whether a batted ball was fair or foul.

B. Whether a runner was safe or out.

C. Whether a pitched ball was a ball or a strike.

D. Whether a pitch was legal or illegal.

E. Whether a runner did or did not touch a base.

F. Whether a runner did or did not leave his base too soon on a caught fly ball.

G. Whether a fly ball was or was not caught legally.

H. Whether it was or was not an infield fly.

I. Whether there was or was not interference or obstruction.

J. Whether the field is or is not fit to continue or resume play.

K. Whether there is or is not sufficient light to continue play.

L. Whether a player or live ball did or did not enter a dead ball area or touch some object or person in a dead ball area.

M. Whether a batted ball did or did not clear the fence in flight.

N. Whether a batted ball was or was not touched by a fielder before clearing the fence in flight.

O. Any other matter involving only the accuracy of the umpire's judgment.

SECTION 2. PROTESTS. There are three types of protests:

A. Misinterpretation of a playing rule - must be made before the next pitch or, if on the last play of the game, before the umpires leave the playing field.

B. Illegal substitute or re-entry - must be made while they are in the game and before the umpires leave the playing field.

C. Ineligible player - can be made any time. Eligibility is the decision of the protest committee. (See ASA Code 201 A 7)

SECTION 3. Protests may involve both a matter of judgment and the interpretation of a rule.

EXAMPLE: With one out and runners on second and third, the batter flies out. The runner on third base tags up after the catch, but the runner on second does not. The runner on third crosses the plate before the ball is played at second base for the third out. The umpire does not allow the run to score. The questions as to whether the runners left their bases before the catch or whether the play at second base was made before the runner on third crossed the plate are solely matters of judgment and are not protestable. It is a misinterpretation of a playing rule and a proper subject for protest however, if the umpire fails to allow the run to score.

SECTION 4.

A. The manager, acting manager or captain of the protesting team shall immediately notify the plate umpire that the game is being played under protest. The plate umpire shall in turn notify the opposing manager and official scorekeeper.

B. To aid in the correct determination of the issue, all interested parties shall take notice of the information, details and conditions surrounding the decision to protest.

SECTION 5. The official written protest must be filed within a reasonable time. In the absence of a league or tournament rule establishing the time limit for filing a protest, a protest should be considered if filed within a reasonable time, depending upon the nature of the call and the difficulty of obtaining the information relevant to the protest.

SECTION 6. The written protest should contain the following information:
A. The date, time and place of the game.
B. The names of the umpires and scorers.
C. The rule and section of the official rules or local rules under which the protest is made.
D. The information, details and conditions pertinent to the decision to protest.
E. All essential facts involved in the matter protested.

SECTION 7. The decision rendered on a protested game must result in one of the following:
A. The protest is considered to be invalid and the game score stands as played.
B. When a protest is determined to be valid because of the misinterpretation of a playing rule, the decision will be corrected and the game shall be replayed from the point at which the incorrect decision was made.
C. When a protest for ineligibility is determined to be valid, the offending team shall forfeit the game being played or the game last played to the offended team.

RULE 10 - UMPIRES

NOTE: Failure of umpires to adhere to Rule 10 shall not be grounds for protest. These are guidelines for umpires.

SECTION 1. POWER AND DUTIES.

The umpires are the representative of the league or organization by which they have been assigned to a particular game and, as such, are authorized and required to enforce each section of these rules. They have the power to order a player, coach, captain or manager to carry out or to omit any act which, in their judgment is necessary to give force and effect to one or all of these rules, and to inflict penalties as herein prescribed, The plate umpire shall have the authority to make decisions on any situations not specifically covered in the rules. The following is the general information for umpires.

A. The umpire will not be a member of either team (i.e., player, coach, manager, officer, scorer or sponsor).

B. The umpire should be sure of the date, time, and place of the game and should arrive at the playing field 20 to 30 minutes ahead of time, start the game at the designated time, and leave the field when the game is over. His jurisdiction begins when he enters the field to check the bats and ends when he leaves the field following the completion of the game.

C. The male and female umpire shall wear a powder blue, short-sleeve shirt, dark navy blue socks and slacks and a cap with white with blue trim ASA letters on the front. The ball bag, jacket and/or sweater (all with the approved logo) must also be dark navy blue, and shoes and belt must be black for both male and female umpires. A T-shirt is optional to wear under the powder blue shirt; however, if one is worn, it must be white. The plate umpire in fast pitch MUST wear a black mask, black padding and black throat protector. (An extended wire protector may be worn in lieu of a throat protector on the mask.)

D. The umpires should introduce themselves to the captains, managers and scorers.

E. The umpires should inspect the playing field boundaries and equipment and clarify all ground rules for the representatives of both teams.

F. Each umpire will have the power to make decisions on violations committed during playing time or during suspension of play.

G. No umpire has the authority to set aside or question decisions made by another umpire within the limits of his respective duties as outlined in these rules.

H. An umpire may consult his associate(s) at any time; however, the final decision will rest with the umpire whose exclusive authority it is to make the decision and who requests the opinion of the other umpire(s).

I. In order to define respective duties, the umpire whose primary responsibility is the judging of balls and strikes will be designated as the PLATE UMPIRE, while the umpire whose primary responsibility is the rendering of base decisions will be designated as the BASE UMPIRE.

J. The plate umpire and base umpire will have equal authority to:

1. Call a runner out for leaving a base too soon.
2. Call TIME for suspension of play.
3. Eject a player, coach, manager or other team member from the game for violation of rules or flagrant misconduct.
4. Call all illegal pitches.
5. Forfeit any game.

K. The umpire will declare the batter or runner out,

without waiting for an appeal for such decision, in all cases where such player is retired in accordance with these rules.

NOTE: Unless appealed to, the umpire will not call a player out for failure to touch a base, for leaving a base too soon on a caught fly ball, for batting out of order, or for making an attempt to go to second after reaching first base, as provided in these rules.

EXCEPTION: Seniors Slow Pitch (Rule 8, Section 10 B)

L. The umpire will not penalize a team for any infraction of a rule when imposing the penalty would be to the advantage of the offending team.

SECTION 2. THE PLATE UMPIRE SHOULD.

A. Take a position behind the catcher. He will have full charge of and be responsible for the proper conduct of the game.

B. Call balls and strikes, unless he requests the help of another umpire.

C. By agreement and in cooperation with the base umpire, makes decisions on plays, fair or foul balls and legally or illegally caught balls. On plays which would necessitate the base umpire leaving the infield in a two umpire system, the plate umpire will assume the duties normally required of the base umpire.

D. Determine and declare whether:
   1. A batter bunts or chops a ball.
   2. A batted ball touches the person or clothing of the batter.
   3. A fly ball is an infield or an outfield fly.

E. Render base decisions as indicated in the Umpire's Manual.

F. Assume all duties when assigned as a single umpire to a game.

SECTION 3. THE BASE UMPIRE SHOULD.

A. Take such positions on the playing field as outlined in the Umpire's Manual.

B. Assist the plate umpire in every way to enforce the rules of the game.

SECTION 4.
RESPONSIBILITIES OF A SINGLE UMPIRE.

If only one umpire is assigned, his duties and jurisdictions will extend to all points. The umpire's starting position for each pitch should be from behind home plate. On each batted ball or play that develops, the umpire must move out from behind the plate and into the infield to obtain the best position for any play that develops.

SECTION 5. CHANGE OF UMPIRES.

Teams may not request a change of umpires during a game unless an umpire is incapacitated by injury or illness.

SECTION 6. UMPIRE'S JUDGMENT.

A. There will be no appeal on any decision of any umpire on the grounds that he was not correct in his conclusion as to whether a batted ball was fair or foul, a runner safe or out, a pitched ball is a ball or strike, or on any play involving accuracy of judgment. No decision rendered by any umpire will be reversed except when he is convinced it is in violation of one of these rules. In case the manager, acting manager or captain of either team does seek reversal of a decision based solely on a point of rules, the umpire whose decision is in question will, if in doubt, confer with his associate(s) before taking any action; but under no circumstances will any player or person, other than the manager, acting manager or captain of either team, have any legal right to protest any decision and seek its reversal

B. Under no circumstances will any umpire seek to reverse a decision made by an associate, nor will any umpire criticize or interfere with the duties of his associate(s) unless asked to do so.

C. The umpire-in-chief may rectify any situation in which the reversal of an umpire's decision or a delayed call by an umpire places a batter-runner, a runner or the defensive team in jeopardy. This correction is not possible after one legal or illegal pitch has been thrown, or after the pitcher and all infielders have clearly vacated their normal fielding positions and have left fair territory on their way to the bench or dugout area.

SECTION 7. SIGNALS.

A. **Safe.** Body upright, eyes on the ball, and arms extended straight out with the palms down. A verbal call of "safe" is made as the arms are snapped to this position from the upper chest.

B. **Safe Sell**. The same as the safe call but as the arms are extended straight out with the palms down a step should be taken towards the play.

C. **Out.** Body upright, eyes on the ball and right arm extended straight up as an extension of the shoulder. As we come to the HAMMER position, the elbow is bent at a 90-degree angle and the fist closed with the fingers facing the right ear. The left arm should be brought to the midsection of the body. A verbal call of "out" is made as the right arm is extended high into the air and continued as the arm drops into the HAMMER position.

D. **Out Sell.** Come to upright position and take a step with left foot directly at the play. Your head should remain in position looking at the play as the upper torso turns perpendicular from the play. Raise right arm with an open hand behind your head into a throwing position as you shuffle your right foot behind the left. Plant right foot and transfer weight, bringing right arm over the top of your head with a closed fist, and make a vigorous "out" call. Finish call by transferring your weight to the left foot while bringing the right foot forward and parallel to the left.

E. **Strike.** Body upright, eyes on the pitcher and right arm extended straight up as an extension of the shoulder. As we come to the HAMMER position, the elbow is bent at a 90-degree angle and the fist is closed with the fingers facing the right ear. The left arm should be brought to the midsection of the body. A verbal call of "strike" is made as the right arm is extended high into the air and continued as the arm drops into the HAMMER position.

F. **Fair Ball.** Body upright, eyes on the ball and point toward fair territory with the arm toward the infield. There is no verbal call on a fair ball, and if the umpire is wearing a mask, it should be in the left hand.

G. **Foul Ball.** On all foul balls, the ball is dead and the dead ball signal should be given preceding the foul ball signal. For the foul ball signal, body should be upright, eyes on the ball, and the arm extended straight out from the shoulder toward foul territory away from the playing field. A verbal call of "foul ball" should be declared as the arm motion is made.

H. **Time Out/Dead Ball/No Pitch.** Body upright and both arms extended high into the air with the palms of the hands open and facing away from the umpire's body. A verbal call of "time out", "dead ball" or "no pitch" is made at the same time the arms are going up.

I. **Play Ball.** Body upright, eyes on the pitcher and the umpire makes a motion toward the pitcher. On a right handed batter use the right hand. On a left-handed batter use the left hand. A verbal call of "play" or "play ball" is made as the umpire motions toward the pitcher.

J. **Hold Up Play.** Body upright and raise either hand with the palm facing the pitcher. On a right-handed batter use the right hand. On a left-handed batter use the left hand. "No pitch" shall be declared if the pitcher pitches while the umpire has a hand in this position.

K. **Delayed Dead Ball.** Body upright, the left arm is extended straight out to the side of the body as an extension of the shoulder and the left hand is in a fist. This position is held long enough for the players to see that the umpire has observed the act that caused this call.

L. **Infield Fly.** Body upright, eyes on the ball and right arm extended high into the air with a closed fist. Make a verbal call of "Infield Fly". If the batted ball is near a foul line, call "Infield Fly if Fair."

M. **Trapped Ball.** Same as safe signal. The umpire makes a verbal call of "safe."

N. **Foul Tip.** Body upright and eyes on the ball. The fingers of both hands are touched together and then the umpire gives the strike signal with no verbal call. This indicates that the bat tipped the ball and was caught by the catcher.

O. **Count.** Body upright. Have eye contact with the pitcher. Both hands are extended high above the head. The fingers are used to indicate the ball and strike count on the batter. Use the fingers of the left hand for balls and the fingers of the right hand for strikes. A verbal description of the count on the batter is given while the hands are overhead. Balls are always mentioned first and strikes second.

P. **Double.** Body upright. Raise the right hand high above the head indicating with two fingers the number of bases awarded. A verbal call of "two bases" is made while the hand remains overhead.

Q. **Home Run.** Body upright. Raise the right hand high above the head with a closed fist. Make a counterclockwise circling motion with the raised fist. A verbal call of "home run" is made at the same time the fist is overhead.

R. **Four-Base Award.** Body upright. Raise the right hand high above the head with four fingers shown. A verbal call of "four-base award" is made at the same time the hand is overhead.

SECTION 8. SUSPENSION OF PLAY.

A. An umpire may suspend play when, in his judgment, conditions justify such action.

B. Play will be suspended whenever the plate umpire leaves his position to brush the plate or to perform other duties not directly connected with the calling of plays.

C. The umpire will suspend play whenever a batter or pitcher steps out of position for a legitimate reason.

D. An umpire will suspend play if a fair batted ball hits him prior to passing an infielder.
EFFECT: The batter-runner is awarded a base hit. No runners are advanced unless forced to advance.

E. An umpire will not call time while any play is in progress, including when a thrown ball hits an umpire.

F. An umpire will not call time after the pitcher has started his windup.

G. In case of injury, time will not be called until all plays in progress have been completed or each runner has been held at his base.

H. Umpires will not suspend play at the request of players, coaches or managers until all action in progress has been completed.

I. (Slow Pitch Only) When, in the judgment of an umpire, all immediate play is apparently completed, he should call time.

SECTION 9. VIOLATIONS AND PENALTIES.

A. Players, coaches, managers or other team members will not make disparaging or insulting remarks to or about opposing players, officials or spectators or commit other acts that could be considered unsportsmanlike conduct.

B. There will be no more than two coaches for each team to give words or signals of assistance and direction to the members of their team while at bat. One should be stationed near first base and the other near third base. Each coach must remain in his coach's box.

C. The penalty for violations by a player is prompt ejection of the offender from the game. For the first offense, a coach or manager may be warned, but for the second offense he is ejected from the game. The offender may remain on the bench. If the act is flagrant or if continued unsportsmanlike conduct comes from the ejected player on the bench, the offender should go directly to the dressing room or leave the grounds for the remainder of the game. Failure to do so will warrant a forfeiture of the game.

RULE 11 - SCORING

NOTE: Failure of official scorer to adhere to Rule 11 shall not be grounds for protest. These are guidelines for the official scorer.

SECTION 1. THE OFFICIAL SCORER SHALL KEEP RECORDS OF EACH GAME AS OUTLINED IN THE FOLLOWING RULES.

He shall have sole authority to make all decisions involving judgment. For example, it is the scorer's responsibility to determine whether a batter-runner's advance to first base is the result of a hit or an error; however, a scorer shall not make a decision which conflicts with the official playing rules or with an umpire's decision.

SECTION 2. THE BOX SCORE.

A. Each player's name and the position or positions he has played shall be listed in the order in which he batted or would have batted had he not been removed or had the game not ended before his turn at bat.

1. (Fast Pitch Only) The designated player (DP) is optional, but if one is used, it must be made known prior to the start of the game and listed on the score sheet in the regular batting order. Ten names will be listed, with the 10th name being the player playing defense only. This 10th player may only bat if he moves to the DP position in the batting order.
   EXCEPTION: See Rule 4, Section 3C.

2. (Slow Pitch Only) The extra player (EP) is optional, but if one is used, it must be made known prior to the start of the game and be listed on the score sheet in the regular batting order. There will be 11 names for men's and women's slow pitch and 12 names for coed slow

---

pitch on the official batting order and all will bat.

3. (ADA Slow Pitch) If the physically challenged player is playing defense only (DEFO), he will be listed last on the score sheet.

B. Each player's batting and fielding record must be tabulated.

1. The first column will show the number of times at bat by each player, but a time at bat will not be charged against the player when:

   (a) He hits a sacrifice fly that scores a runner.

   (b) He is awarded a base on balls.

   (c) (Fast Pitch Only) He hits a sacrifice bunt.

   (d) (Fast Pitch Only) He is hit by a pitched ball.

   (e) (Fast Pitch Only) He hits a sacrifice slap hit.

   NOTE: A slap hit is defined as a fake bunt followed by a controlled swing and resulting in the runner(s) advancing, as in the case of a sacrifice bunt.

2. The second column will show the number of runs scored by each player.

3. The third column will show the number of base hits made by each player. A base hit is a batted ball that permits the batter to reach base safely:

   (a) On a fair ball which settles on the ground, clears the fence or strikes the fence before being touched by a fielder.

   (b) On a fair ball which is hit with such force or such slowness or which takes such an unnatural bounce that it is impossible to field with ordinary effort in time to retire the runner.

      (c) When a fair ball which has not been touched by a fielder becomes dead because of touching the person or clothing of a runner or umpire.

      (d) When a fielder unsuccessfully attempts to retire a preceding runner and in the scorer's judgment, the batter-runner would not have been retired at first base by perfect fielding.

4. The fourth column will show the number of opponents put out by each player.

      (a) A putout is credited to a fielder each time he:

          (1) Catches a fly ball or line drive.

          (2) Catches a thrown ball which retires a batter-runner or runner.

          (3) Touches a runner with ball when the runner is off the base to which he is entitled.

          (4) Is nearest the ball when a runner is declared out for being struck by a fair batted ball or for interference with a fielder, or when a runner is called out for being in violation of Rule 8, Sections 8E, J, S, or T.

      (b) A putout is credited to the catcher:

          (1) When a third strike is called.

          (2) (Slow Pitch Only) When the batter bunts or chops the ball.

          (3) When the batter fails to bat in correct order.

          (4) When the batter interferes with the catcher.

          (5) (Slow Pitch Only) When the batter

hits a third strike foul ball.

> (6) (Slow Pitch Only) When a batter hits a home run in excess of the limit.

5. The fifth column shall show the number of assists made by each player. An assist shall be credited:

   (a) To each player who handles the ball in any series of plays which results in the putout of a runner or batter-runner. Only one assist shall be given to any player who handles the ball on any putout. The player who makes the putout in a run-down or similar type play shall be credited with both an assist and a putout.

   (b) To each player who handles or throws the ball in such a manner that a putout would have resulted except for an error of a teammate.

   (c) To each player who, by deflecting a batted ball, aids in a putout.

   (d) To each player who handles the ball on a play which results in a runner or batter-runner being called out for interference or for running out of the baseline.

6. The sixth column will show the number of errors made by each player. Errors are recorded:

   (a) For each player who commits a misplay which prolongs the turn at bat of the batter or the life of a present runner.

   (b) For the fielder who fails to touch a base after receiving a thrown ball to retire a runner on a force out, or when a runner is compelled to return to a base, and pro-

vided the thrown ball could be caught by
the fielder with ordinary effort.
    (c) For the catcher if a batter is awarded first
        base because of catcher obstruction.
    (d) For the fielder who fails to complete a
        double play because of a dropped ball.
    (e) For a fielder if a runner advances a base
        because of said fielder's failure to catch,
        stop or try to stop a ball accurately thrown
        to a base, provided there was occasion for
        the throw. When more than one player
        could receive the throw, the scorer must
        determine which player gets the error.

SECTION 3. A BASE HIT shall not be scored:
    A. When a runner is forced out on a batted ball or would
       have been forced out except for a fielding error.
    B. When a player fielding a batted ball retires a preced-
       ing runner with ordinary effort.
    C. When a fielder fails in an attempt to retire a preceding
       runner and, in the scorer's judgment, the batter-run-
       ner could have been retired at first base.

SECTION 4. A RUN BATTED IN is a run scored
    because of:
    A. A safe hit.
    B. A sacrifice bunt (Fast Pitch), a sacrifice slap hit (Fast
       Pitch) or a sacrifice fly (Fast Pitch and Slow Pitch).
    C. An infield putout or fielder's choice.
    D. A runner forced home because of obstruction, a hit
       batter or a base on balls.
    E. A home run and all runs scored as a result.
    F. Subject to the provisions of Rule 11, Section 4G,
       when the batter ends a game with a safe hit which dri-
       ves in as many runs as are necessary to put his team in
       the lead, He shall be credited with only as many bases

on his hit as are advanced by the runner who scores
the winning run, and then only if the batter runs out
his hit for as many bases as are advanced by the runner who scores the winning run.
G. When the batter ends a game with a home run hit out
of the playing field, any runners on base are entitled
to score.

SECTION 5. A PITCHER SHALL BE CREDITED WITH A WIN.

A. When a starting pitcher has pitched at least four
innings and his team is not only in the lead when he
is replaced but remains in the lead for the remainder
of the game.
B. When a starting pitcher has pitched at least three
innings and his team scores more runs than the
opposing team in a game that is terminated after five
innings of play, or in a game that is terminated after
his team has scored more runs in four or more innings
than the opposing team has scored in five or more
innings and provided that his team is not only in the
lead if he is replaced after three innings of pitching
but remains in the lead for the remainder of the game.

SECTION 6. Regardless of the number of innings he has
pitched, a pitcher shall be charged with a loss if he is
replaced when his team is behind in the score and fails to
tie the score or gain the lead thereafter.

SECTION 7. THE SUMMARY shall list the following
items in this order:
A. The score by innings and the final score.
B. The runs batted in and by whom.
C. Two-base hits and by whom.
D. Three-base hits and by whom.
E. Home runs and by whom.

F. Sacrifice flies and by whom.

G. Double plays and players participating in them.

H. Triple plays and players participating in them.

I. Number of bases on balls charged to each pitcher.

J. Number of strike outs by each pitcher.

K. Number of hits and runs allowed by each pitcher.

L. The name of the winning pitcher.

M. The name of the losing pitcher.

N. The time of the game.

O. The names of the umpires and scorers.

P. (Fast Pitch Only) Stolen bases and by whom.
NOTE: This includes a batter advancing to second base on an awarded base on balls.

Q. (Fast Pitch Only) Sacrifice bunts and by whom.

R. (Fast Pitch Only) The names of batters hit by a pitched ball and the names of the pitchers who hit them.

S. (Fast Pitch Only) The number of wild pitches charged to each pitcher.

T. (Fast Pitch Only) The number of passed balls charged to each catcher.

SECTION 8. (Fast Pitch Only) A stolen base is credited to a runner whenever he advances one base unaided by a hit, putout, force out, fielder's choice, passed ball, wild pitch, an error, illegal pitch or obstruction.

SECTION 9. All records of a forfeited game will be included in the official records except that of a pitcher's won-lost record.

SECTION 10. TIE BREAKER RULE..
In scoring, the run scored by the player starting as a runner at second base shall be charged to the defensive team and not the pitcher. Depending on the judgement of the official scorekeeper, a run scored by any other player will be charged to the pitcher's ERA.

Softball
Official Rules

Part Two
POINTS
OF EMPHASIS

1. **APPEALS.**
    A. **Types.**
        1. Missing a base.
        2. Leaving a base on a caught fly ball before the ball is first touched.
        3. Batting out of order.
        4. Attempting to advance to second base after making the turn at first base.
        5. (Seniors) Ineligible Courtesy Runner.
    B. **Alive.** In all games an appeal may be made during a live ball by touching the base missed or left too soon on a caught fly ball, or by tagging the runner committing the violation if he is still on the playing field.
    C. **Dead.** The dead ball appeal may be made in all games once time has been granted. Any infielder, with or without the ball, may make a verbal appeal on a runner missing a base or leaving a base too soon on a caught fly ball. The administering umpire should then make a decision on the play.
    D. **May Not Return.** A runner may not return to touch a missed base or one left too soon on a caught fly ball if:
        1. He has left the field of play.
        2. A following runner has scored, or
        3. He is standing on a base beyond the base he left too soon and time out has been called by the umpire, or the ball becomes dead.
        NOTE: If the runner is between any two bases and attempting to return to the base left too soon, he can continue (Rule 8, Section 3 A).
    E. **When.** Appeals must be made (1) before the next legal or illegal pitch, (2) before the pitcher and all infielders have clearly vacated their normal fielding positions and have left fair territory on their way to the bench or dugout area, or (3) on the last play of the

game, an appeal can be made until the umpires leave the field of play.

F. **Advance.** Runners may advance during a live ball appeal play. If the ball is not dead in fast pitch, each runner may leave his base when (1) the pitcher no longer has possession of the ball within eight feet of the pitcher's plate, or (2) when the pitcher makes a play on any runner (a fake throwing motion is considered a play). If time out is requested for an appeal, the umpire should grant it in either fast pitch or slow pitch, and runners may not advance until the next pitch.

G. **More Than One Appeal.** More than one appeal play may be made but guessing games should not be allowed.

EXAMPLE: The runner misses second base by a step but just touches the corner of third base. Even though an appeal is made at third (the umpire called the runner safe), an appeal may be made at second on the same runner.

H. **Awards.** An appeal must be honored even if the base missed was before or after an award.

I. **Plate and Missed Tag**. If a runner misses home plate and the catcher misses the tag, the umpire should hesitate slightly. If no tag is made, he should declare the runner safe. If an appeal play is then made by tagging either the runner or home plate, the umpire should then make a decision on this appeal play.

J. **Force Out.** If an appeal is honored at a base to which a runner was forced to advance and the out is a force out, no runs would score if it was the third out. If a forced runner, after touching the next base, retreats for any reason towards the base he had last occupied, the force play is reinstated and he may again be put out if the defense tags the base to which he is forced.

NOTE: There cannot be a force out if the batter does not become a batter-runner or runner.

K. **Tag-Ups**. If a runner leaves a base too soon on a caught fly ball and returns in an attempt to retag, this is considered a time play and not a force out. If the appeal is the third out, all runs scored by runners in advance of the appealed runner and scored ahead of the legal appeal would count.

L. **Missing First Base Before the Throw Arrives**. If a runner passes first base before the throw arrives, he is considered to have touched the base unless an appeal play is made.

M. **Fourth Out Appeal**. An appeal may be made after the third out as long as it is made properly. (i.e., One out with runner on first and third. The batter hits a fly ball that is caught. Each runner leaves his base before the caught ball is touched. An appeal is made at first base for the third out. The defensive team then makes an appeal at third base before the infielders leave the infield. The runner on third would then be declared out also, and the run would not count.

2. BALL ROTATION PROCEDURE.

A ball rotation procedure is used in championship play and many local associations are now following the same procedure. Listed below is this procedure.

The pitcher has a choice of which ball to use at the start of each inning. If both balls do not get into play in the first half of the first inning, the pitcher in the bottom half of the first inning MUST throw the unused ball. No choice is offered.

The current game ball must be used until such time as it goes out of play or becomes unplayable. When the ball goes out of play, the umpire will throw a new ball to the pitcher. If the pitcher does not like that ball, remove it from the game and give him another ball. An umpire should never take a ball back from the pitcher and put it in his ball bag unless it is at the start of the inning when the pitcher is selecting his game ball.

After an inning is completed, the ball should be returned to the vicinity of the pitching plate by the team leaving the field or the umpire. The pitcher taking the field now has a ball with which to start the next half inning. The pitcher may request the other ball from the plate umpire, but should throw the first ball to the umpire prior to receiving the second ball. He should not have both game balls in his possession when making his choice.

3. **BATTING OUT OF THE BATTER'S BOX.**
   In order for the batter to be called out for batting out of the batter's box, **one foot or both feet must be on the ground completely outside the lines of the box when contact is made with the ball.** The lines of the batter's box are considered inside the box. The batter is to be called out if any part of a foot is touching home plate when he contacts the ball even though he may be touching the lines of the batter's box.

   Hitting the ball while out of the batter's box should be called immediately. The ball is dead. The batter is out whether the ball is fair or foul. In cases where there are no batter's box lines evident, good judgement must be used and the benefit of any doubt must go to the batter.

4. **CATCHER'S BOX.**
   The catcher's box, as described in Rule 2, Section 3 D, is 10 feet in length from the rear outside corners of the batter's boxes.

(Slow Pitch Only) The catcher may not have any part of his body or equipment touching the ground outside the lines of the catcher's box until the ball is batted, touches the ground or plate, or reaches the catcher's box. It is a violation of Rule 6, Section 6 A and an illegal pitch if the catcher touches the ground outside the lines of the catcher's box, including home plate. The intent of this rule is to prevent catcher's obstruction. Even if the catcher is legally within the catcher's box, he may not obstruct the batter.

(Fast Pitch Only) Catchers must remain in the catcher's box until the pitch is released when intentionally walking a batter. During a regular pitch to a batter, should the batter be in the front of the batter's box, the catcher can move closer to the plate without penalty. At all times, the catcher must still avoid catcher's obstruction as the batter legally has the right to the entire batter's box.

Obstruction does not require contact between the catcher and the bat or batter. The umpire's request for the catcher to move farther away from the batter to avoid injury or obstruction should always be obeyed. (See catcher obstruction under POE #23.)

5. **CHECK SWING/BUNT STRIKE.**
   Normally, there are four areas which constitute whether or not the batter has swung at the ball or checked the swing. (1) Did he roll his wrists? (2) Did he swing through the ball and bring the bat back, unless the batter draws the bat back before the pitch arrives? (3) Was the bat out in front of the body? (4) Did he make an attempt to hit the pitch?

   On a bunt attempt where the batter puts the bat across the plate, unless the batter moves the bat towards the ball, a strike would not be called if the ball is out of the strike zone.

In each situation, the umpire thinks in terms of priorities. First, was the pitch in the strike zone? If so, it is simply a strike. Second, did the batter swing at the pitched ball or in the case of a bunt attempt, did he move the bat toward the pitched ball? In either case, it is the plate umpire's call. If in doubt or if blocked out, he will call the pitch a ball. Umpires will not call the pitch a strike unless it was in the strike zone or the batter swung at the ball. If the umpire calls the pitch a ball and the catcher requests help, the umpire should ask for help. **On a missed bunt attempt with two strikes, the dropped third strike rule will apply. (Rule 8, Section 1 B)**

6. **CONFERENCES.**
   A. **Defensive.** A defensive charged conference takes place when the defense requests a suspension of play for any reason, and a representative enters the playing field and confers with the pitcher. The intent of this rule is to reduce delays in the game. **It is also a conference if the team representative confers with another player who, prior to a pitch being thrown, confers with the pitcher.** The umpire should advise the team representative when he declares a charged conference. The penalty for a second charged conference with the same pitcher in one inning is removal of the pitcher from the pitching position for the duration of the game. If the pitcher returns to the pitching position after being removed and one pitch has been thrown, the pitcher is ejected from the game.

   The following are not defensive conferences:
   1. If the team representative informs an umpire prior to crossing the foul line that he is remov-

ing the pitcher, and he does so.

2. Shouting instructions from the dugout area to the pitcher.

3. If a dugout representative confers with a pitcher during a charged offensive conference and is ready to play ball when the offense is ready.

4. A manager playing in the game may confer with the pitcher and is not charged; however, an umpire may control repeated meetings between a playing manager and a pitcher by first issuing a warning and then ejecting the manager.

B. **Offensive.** An offensive charged conference occurs when an offensive team requests a suspension of play and is granted time by an umpire to permit a team representative (usually the manager or coach) to confer with a batter and/or runner(s). Only one such conference is allowed per inning. The umpires should refuse to grant the second conference.

PENALTY: If the offensive team insists on holding a second conference in an inning after being informed by the umpire that it is not permitted, the umpire should eject the team representative from the game. The following are not offensive conferences:

1. A team representative confers with a batter and/or runner(s) during a defensive charged conference and is ready to play when the defense is.

2. If the pitcher is putting on a warm-up jacket.

7. **DELAYED DEAD BALL.**

There are six situations when a violation of a rule occurs, it is recognized by an umpire and the ball remains live until the conclusion of the play. These situations are:

A. An illegal pitch. (Rule 6, Section 1-8 • Fast Pitch and Modified Pitch) (Rule 6, Section 1-7 • Slow Pitch and

16-Inch Slow Pitch)
B. Catcher's obstruction. (Rule 8, Section 1 D)
C. Plate umpire interference. (Rule 8, Section 7 F)
D. Obstruction. (Rule 8, Section 6 B)
E. Batted or thrown ball hit with detached equipment.
   (Rule 8, Section 6 F)
F. Runner at third or first base assisted by a coach on a
   tag up. (Rule, 8, Section 8 M)
NOTE: Once the entire play is completed in each situa-
   tion, the proper enforcement should be made. In (F),
   a double play could be called. One out on the coach
   assisting the runner and the second on the caught fly
   ball.

8. DELIBERATELY CRASHING INTO A FIELDER WITH THE BALL. (Interference)

In order to prevent injury and protect the defensive
player attempting to make a play on a runner, the runner
must be called out if he remains on his feet and deliberately, with great force, crashes into a defensive player
holding the ball and waiting to apply a tag. In order to
prevent a deliberate crash ruling, the runner can slide,
jump over the top of the defender holding the ball, go
around the defender (if outside the three-foot lane, the
runner would be called out), or return to the previous
base touched.
NOTE: If the act is determined to be flagrant, the
offender will be ejected. A runner may slide into the
fielder.
A. When a runner is called out for deliberately crashing
   into a fielder holding the ball, **the ball becomes dead**.
   Each runner must return to the last base touched at
   the time of interference.
B. If, in A above, the runner deliberately crashed into a
   fielder holding the ball before he was put out and, in

the judgement of the umpire, it was an attempt to break up an obvious double play, **the immediate succeeding runner will also be declared out under Rule 8, Section 8 J).**

C. If the deliberate crash occurs after the runner was called out, **the runner closest to home plate will be declared out under Rule 8, Section 8 Q.**

D. If an obstructed runner deliberately crashes into a fielder holding the ball, **the obstruction call will be ignored** and the runner will be called out under Rule 8, Section 8 R. An award of this type under Rule 8, Section 6 B (1 and 2) does not give the runner the right to violate Rule 8, Section 8 R.

9. **DESIGNATED PLAYER OR DP (Fast Pitch Only).** This individual can be listed in any of the nine spots in the batting order. The player listed number 10 in the lineup, who plays defense only, will be called the DEFO.

A. Any of the starting 10 players may be withdrawn and re-enter the game one time.

B. Only nine players may bat; however, defensive players may play any position any time on defense without penalty. DPs are not limited to one defensive position.

C. No one is considered to have left the game until he has been removed from the batting order.
EXCEPTION: The DEFO is considered to have left the game any time he is substituted for, or the DP plays defense for him.

D. If the DP plays defense for some player other than the DEFO, in reality the other player only bats and becomes a temporary DP.

E. The DP and DEFO may never be on offense at the same time.

F. The DEFO may never play offense only.

G. The DEFO may only enter the game on offense in the original DP position.

H. The DP may never play defense only.

I. The DP and DEFO may re-enter the game one time, just like any other starting player.

10. **EQUIPMENT ON THE PLAYING FIELD.**

No loose equipment, miscellaneous items or a detached part of a player's uniform, other than that being legally used in the game at the time, should be within playable territory. Official equipment which may be within playable territory with no penalty includes the batter's bat, the catcher's mask, umpire paraphernalia, any helmet which has inadvertently fallen off on an offensive or defensive player during the course of play or any equipment belonging to a person assigned to the game. Loose gloves, hats, helmets, jackets, balls (including the on-deck batter's bat), or any other loose equipment, miscellaneous item or detached uniform part which are within playable territory and are not being legally used in the game at the time could cause a blocked ball or interference.

A. **Thrown Ball.**

1. If a thrown ball hits loose equipment belonging to the team at bat, **a dead ball is declared immediately.** If such action interferes with a play, **interference is ruled**. The runner closest to home at the time of the interference shall be declared out, the ball is dead, and each runner must return to the last base touched prior to the thrown ball hitting the loose equipment.

   NOTE: If no apparent play is obvious, no one is called out, but all runners must return to the last base touched at the time of the dead ball declaration.

2. If the loose equipment belongs to the team in

the field, it becomes a blocked ball and the
overthrow rule applies.

B. **Batted Ball.**
   1. A batted foul ball touching loose equipment is a
      foul ball.
   2. A batted fair ball touching loose equipment
      belonging to (a) the offense is considered a **dead
      ball and runners return, unless they are forced
      to advance when the batter-runner is awarded
      first base on the base hit** or (b) the defense is
      considered a dead ball and **all runners, includ-
      ing the batter-runner, are awarded two bases
      from their position at the time of the pitch.**

11. **EXTRA PLAYER OR EP (Slow Pitch Only).**
    If a team uses the EP, it must be on the lineup card at
    the start of the game, and the team must end the game
    with 11 players or forfeit.
    EXCEPTION: short-handed team ruling.

    All 11 players bat but only 10 play defense. Changes with
    the defensive players may be made at any time; however,
    the batting order may not change. (e.g., The EP may sit
    on the bench one inning, play third base one inning, play
    outfield one inning, sit on the bench again and then play
    first base. All would be legal as long as the EP remained in
    his same position in the batting order. This would be the
    same for any of the starting 11 players.).

    Any of the starting 11 players may leave the game once
    and re-enter. A starting player and his substitute may not
    be in the game at the same time. If this occurs, the man-
    ager and the player listed in the wrong spot in the batting
    order are ejected by the umpire.

12. FAKE TAG.

A. A fake tag occurs when a fielder without the ball deceives the runner by impeding his progress (i.e., causing him to slide, slow down or stop running).

1. Obstruction is called when a fake tag is made as mentioned above. The umpire shall give the delayed dead ball signal and let the play continue to its completion. The obstructed runner, and each runner affected by the obstruction, will always be awarded the base or bases he would have reached if there had not been any obstruction under Rule 8, Section 6 B 3. Remember, each runner is awarded a base or bases only, if in the judgement of the umpire, he would have made the base or bases had there not been any obstruction.

2. **The umpire should rule obstruction on a fake tag.** Continued fake tags should result in ejections. In flagrant cases where the sliding player gets hurt, the offending player should be ejected without warning.

3. If a fielder fakes a tag but the runner continues on to the next base without sliding or breaking stride, there is not a rule violation. Obstruction is the act of a fielder in the base path without the ball impeding the progress of a runner. In this case, the progress was not impeded. A warning may still be given.

13. FALLING OVER THE FENCE ON A CATCH.

The fence is an extension of the playing field, making it legal for a player to climb and make the catch. If he catches a ball in the air and his momentum carries him through or over the fence, the catch is good, the batter-runner is out, the ball is dead, and with fewer than two

outs, all runners are advanced one base without liability
to be put out. Guidelines are (1) if he catches the ball
before he touches the ground outside the playing area,
the catch is legal, or (2) if he catches the ball **after** he
touches the ground outside the playing area, it is not a
catch. If a portable fence is used which is collapsible and
a defensive player is standing on the fence, it is ruled a
good catch.

14. **HITTING THE BALL A SECOND TIME.**
    When an umpire considers the act of a batter hitting the
    ball a second time, he should place the act into one of
    three categories.
    A. If the bat is in the hands of the batter when the ball
       comes in contact with it, and the batter is in the bat-
       ter's box, it is a foul ball. If an entire foot of the batter
       is completely outside the batter's box, he is out. When
       in doubt, don't guess the batter out. Call it a foul ball.
    B. If the bat is out of the batter's hands (dropped or
       thrown) and it hits the ball in fair territory, the ball is
       dead and the batter-runner is out. If the ball hits the
       bat on the ground, the batter is not out. The umpire
       should then determine whether the ball is fair or foul
       based on the fair/foul rule. If the ball rolls against the
       bat in fair territory, it remains live. If it stops or is
       touched in fair territory, it is a fair ball. If it touches
       the bat in fair territory and then rolls to foul ground
       and stops, it is a foul ball. If the ball rolls against the
       bat in foul territory, it is a foul ball regardless.
    C. If a batter swings and misses the pitched ball but (a)
       accidentally hits it on the follow-through, (b) inten-
       tionally hits it on the second swing, or (c) hits the ball
       after it bounces off the catcher or his mitt, the ball is
       dead whether hit fair or foul, and it is called a foul ball.
       If it is the third strike in slow pitch, the batter is out.

15. IMAGINARY LINE OR DEAD BALL AREA.

When a fielder carries a live ball into a dead ball area, the ball becomes dead and a base or bases are awarded to all baserunners. If the act is unintentional, the award is one base. If the act is intentional, the award is two bases. The base award is governed from the last base legally touched at the time the ball became dead.

If a chalk line is used to determine an out-of-play area, the line is considered in play. If a fielder is touching the line, he is considered in the field of play and may make a legal catch or throw. If either foot is on the ground completely in dead ball territory (not touching the line), the ball becomes dead and no play may be made.

If a player has one foot inside the line or touching the line, and another foot in the air at the time the catch is made, the catch is good and the batter is out. If the fielder then steps into a dead ball area (foot on the ground), the ball becomes dead and all baserunners are awarded one base from the last base touched when the ball became dead.

16. INTENTIONALLY DROPPED BALL.

The ball cannot be intentionally dropped unless the fielder has actually caught and then dropped it. Merely guiding the ball to the ground should not be considered an intentionally dropped ball.

17. INTENTIONALLY THROWN BALL OUT OF PLAY.

Defensive players who intentionally throw the ball out of play in order to prevent a runner from returning to a previous base will be penalized by awarding all runners two bases from the last base touched when the ball left the fielder's hand. Normal award would be from the original base if a runner is returning to the original base. (Rule 8, Section 6 K)

18. **INTENTIONAL WALK (Fast Pitch Only).**

The ball is live during an intentional walk in fast pitch. All defensive players must be in fair territory until the pitch is released, except the catcher, who must remain in the catcher's box, and the pitcher, who must be in a legal pitching position at the start of each pitch. If they do not position themselves in fair territory, an illegal pitch should be called for each pitch thrown while any member of the defense is standing in foul territory. In fast pitch, the pitches must be thrown to the catcher.

19. **INTENTIONAL WALK (Slow Pitch Only).**

Because the ball is dead when it crosses the plate and no play may be made, it is permissible for the batter to be walked intentionally if the umpire is notified by the pitcher. **If two successive batters are to be walked,** the plate umpire will not award the second intentional walk until the first batter reaches first base. (Rule 8, Section 1 C 2)

20. **INTERFERENCE.**

Interference is defined as the act of an **offensive** player or team member which impedes, hinders or confuses a defensive player attempting to execute a play. It may be in the form of physical contact, verbal distraction, visual distraction, or any type of distraction which would hinder the fielder in the execution of the play. Defensive players must be given the opportunity to field the ball **anywhere** on the playing field or throw the ball without being hindered.

A. Baserunning interference includes: a runner or batter-runner who interferes with a fielder; a runner or batter-runner who is hit by a fair untouched batted ball;

and a thrown ball which strikes any illegal loose equipment, detached part of a uniform or miscellaneous item left in playable territory by the offensive team.

1. When a runner interferes with a fielder, the umpire must determine if the interference occurred before or after the runner who interfered was put out and then apply the proper rule.

2. When a baserunner is hit by a fair batted ball, it is interference if it occurred **before** it passed an infielder (excluding the pitcher) or **after** it passed an infielder (if another fielder had a chance to make an out), and provided the runner was not in contact with the base. It is not interference if the batted ball touched or was touched by a player before it hit the runner, or if the runner was standing in foul territory.

3. A runner could be standing on a base and a defensive player bumps the runner while watching the flight of the ball. If the defensive player fails to make a catch on a catchable ball, it is the umpire's judgement whether interference should or should not be called. The rule provides that a runner must vacate any space needed by a fielder to make a play on a batted ball, unless the runner has contact with a legally occupied base when the hindrance occurs. In this case, the runner should not be called out unless the hindrance is intentional.

4. For deliberate crash interference, refer to POE #8.

B. Batter interference occurs while the batter is at bat and before he hits the ball. It occurs in fast pitch when the batter intentionally interferes with the catcher's throw on an attempted steal or when he interferes with the catcher on a play at the plate. The batter's box is not a sanctuary for the batter when a play is being made at the plate. It could also occur when a batter releases his bat in such a manner that it hits the catcher and prevents him from making a play. If the batter merely drops his bat and the catcher trips over it, there is no interference.

C. On-deck batters may be charged with interference if they interfere with a throw or a fielder's opportunity to make an out on a fly ball.

D. Coach's interference occurs when a base coach runs toward home and draws a throw, when he interferes with a fielder attempting to catch or throw a ball, or when he aids a runner. The coach's box is not a sanctuary.

E. Spectator interference occurs when a spectator enters the field and interferes with a play or reaches onto the field from the stands and prevents a fielder from catching a fly ball in the field of play. It is not interference if the fielder reaches into the stands. The field belongs to the fielder and the stands belong to the spectator.

F. Umpire interference occurs (1) (Fast Pitch & Slow Pitch) when an umpire is hit by a fair, untouched batted ball before it passes an infielder (excluding the pitcher) or after it passes an infielder (including the pitcher) and another fielder had a chance to make an out. The batter-runner is awarded first base (exception to the statement that someone must be called out on interference). (2) (Fast Pitch Only) when an umpire interferes with a catcher's attempt to put out a baserunner stealing. It is interference only if the baserunner is not put out, in which case he is returned to his base. In no other case is umpire interference ruled.

When batter, batter-runner, runner, on-deck batter or coach interference occurs, the ball is dead, someone must be called out, and each other runner must return to the last base touched at the time of the interference.

21. **LOOK-BACK RULE (Fast Pitch Only) (Rule 8 Section 8 U).**

When a runner is legitimately off his base after a pitch, or as a result of a batter completing his turn at bat, he must immediately attempt to advance to the next base or immediately return to the base left while the pitcher has the ball within the eight-foot radius of the pitcher's plate. **The responsibility is completely on the runner.** There is no obligation on the pitcher to look, fake or throw.

A. Failure to immediately proceed to the next base or return to his original base after the pitcher has the ball within the circle will result in the runner being declared out.

B. Once the runner has returned to any base for any reason, he will be declared out if he leaves said base unless (1) a play is made on him or another runner, (2) the pitcher leaves the circle or drops the ball, or (3) the pitcher releases the ball to the batter.

C. If two runners are off base and two different umpires call each runner out, they must determine which runner was called out first and return the other runner to the base he left. It is not possible to obtain two outs on this rule.

A base on balls or a dropped third strike is treated as a batted ball as long as the batter-runner continues past first base. For scoring purposes, when he advances to second base, it is considered a stolen base. If he stops at first base, however, and then steps off the base after the

---

pitcher has the ball within the circle, he is **out.**

If, after the pitcher has the ball within the circle, the runner starts back to his original base or forward to another base and then stops or reverses direction, he is out, unless the pitcher makes a play on him. When a play is made on a runner, he may stop or reverse his direction.

The runner is out if he stands off his base and does not immediately attempt to advance or return after the pitcher has the ball within the circle.

If the pitcher throws the ball from within the circle, carries it outside the circle, sets it on the ground, or otherwise loses possession of it, including handing it to another player, it is interpreted as **making a play** and runners on base may leave at their own risk, provided time is not out. A fake throw is also considered **making a play.** The throwing arm must be raised on a fake throw and an actual movement forward must be made. Just raising the arm is not considered a fake throw.

NOTE: Being in the eight-foot circle is defined as both feet within or partially within the lines. The pitcher is not considered in the circle if either foot is completely outside the lines.

---

22. MEDIA COVERAGE.
Media authorized by the tournament committee can be on the playing field but must not use tripods. All media personnel must be able to move to avoid being hit by an overthrown or batted ball. Should they accidentally be hit, the ball remains live. All photographic equipment must be on the photographer. No equipment can be left on the ground.

---

23. OBSTRUCTION.

Obstruction is the act of a fielder (1) not in possession of the ball, (2) not in the act of fielding a batted ball, or (3) not about to receive a thrown ball which impedes the progress of a batter-runner or runner who is legally running the bases.

NOTE: In defining "not about to receive a thrown ball," the ball must be between the advancing runner and the defensive player about to make the catch and play. If the ball is outside this area and a collision occurs, obstruction is ruled. If the ball is within this area and a collision occurs, it is neither obstruction nor interference and the ball remains live.

Whenever obstruction occurs, whether a play is being made on a runner or not, the umpire will declare obstruction and signal a delayed dead ball. The ball will remain live. If the obstructed runner is put out prior to reaching the base he would have reached had there not been obstruction, a dead ball is called and the obstructed runner, and each other runner affected by the obstruction, will be awarded the base(s) he would have reached, in the umpire's judgement, had there not been obstruction. An obstructed runner may never be called out between two bases where he is obstructed. If he is tagged between the same two bases, the obstructed runner would either be awarded the forward base or returned to the last base touched.

When an obstructed runner is awarded a base he would have made had there been no obstruction and a preceding runner is on that base, time will be called. The obstructed runner will be awarded that base and the runner occupying it will be entitled to the next base without liability to be put out.

It should also be clear that when saying "a runner cannot be called out between the two bases he was obstructed" does not pertain when another violation is being played upon. (e.g., A runner leaving second base too soon on a fly ball is returning after the ball is caught and is obstructed between second base and third base. If the runner would not have made it back to second base prior to the throw arriving, he would remain out.)

If the obstructed runner is put out after passing the base he would have reached had there not been obstruction, he is running at his own risk and, if tagged, would be called out. The ball remains live and other plays may be made.

When the runner is obstructed during a **rundown**, a delayed dead ball is called. If the runner is tagged out after being obstructed, time is called, and he is awarded the base he would have made had there been no obstruction. If the ball is overthrown after the obstruction, the runner may advance. He may not be called out between the two bases where he was obstructed.

If other runners are advancing when an umpire calls time following a play on an obstructed runner, a rule of thumb for placement of the other runners is: If they have not reached half way to the next base, they must return to the previous base. However, if they have advanced over half way, they are allowed to advance to the next base.

Catcher obstruction is a delayed dead ball call. Should catcher obstruction be called when the batter hits the ball, and if he reaches first base safely, and if all other runners have advanced at least one base, the obstruction is cancelled. All action as a result of the batted ball stands. If he does not reach first base or if one of the other runners does not advance at least one base, the manager of the offensive team has the option of taking the result of the play or awarding the batter first base and advancing other runners only if they are forced because of the award.

24. OVER-RUNNING FIRST BASE.

After over-running first base, the batter-runner may legally turn to his left or his right when returning to the base. If any attempt is made to advance to second, regardless of whether he is in fair or foul territory, he is liable for an appeal out if tagged by a defensive player with the ball while off the base.

25. OVERTHROWS.

Runners are always awarded two bases on overthrows which **go out of play or become blocked.** Irregardless of who made the throw, two bases are awarded from the last base touched at the time the ball **left the hand.**

Direction of runners has no bearing on the award. (i.e., When an overthrow is made on a runner returning to a base, he is awarded two bases from that base. If he was returning to first base and the throw was from the outfield and it left the outfielder's hand before the runner got back to first base, the runner would be awarded third base.)

If a runner touches the next base and returns to his original base, the original base he left is considered the last base touched for purposes of an overthrow award.

The award of bases is determined by the position of the front runner if two runners are between the same bases at the time of the award. Two runners between first and second will be awarded second and third; however, if two runners are between second and third, both will be awarded home.

When a fielder loses possession of the ball on an attempted tag and the ball then enters the dead ball area or becomes blocked, all runners are awarded one base from the last base touched at the time the ball entered the dead ball area or became blocked.

(Fast Pitch Only) On pitched balls going out of play, the runners are awarded one base from the last base touched at the time of the pitch. If a batter receives a base on balls and the fourth ball gets away from the catcher and goes out of play, he will be awarded first base only.

26. **PITCHING (Fast Pitch Only).**
    There are six basic features in the pitching rule. They are:
    A. **Contact With the Pitcher's Plate. Male adult and male Junior Olympic pitchers** may have only one foot in contact with the pitcher's plate. The non-pivot foot may be on or behind it. Both feet must be within the 24-inch length of said plate. **Female adult and female Junior Olympic pitchers** must have both feet in contact with the pitcher's plate and within the 24-inch length of said plate.
    B. **Signal.** A signal must be taken by the pitcher while one or both feet are in contact with the pitcher's plate, the ball is held in one hand only and the hands are clearly separated. The ball held in one hand may be in front of or behind the body. Taking a signal prevents a pitcher from walking onto the pitcher's plate and putting the batter at a disadvantage by throwing a quick pitch.
    C. **Preliminary to Windup.** In the **male adult and male Junior Olympic competition**, if the pitcher takes the signal with both feet on the plate and he wants to pitch with the non-pivot foot starting behind the plate, he may step or slide this foot backwards prior to

bringing the two hands together, when simultaneously bringing the two hands together or after bring the two hands together. **Female adult and female Junior Olympic pitchers** must keep both feet in contact with the pitcher's plate during the entire preliminary process. Both: After taking the signal, the ball must be taken in both hands and held for a minimum of one second and not more than 10 seconds. The pitcher may begin the pitch once the hands are brought together. During this entire period, the pivot foot must remain in contact with the pitcher's plate. No rocking movement which pulls the pivot foot off the pitcher's plate is allowed. If the pivot foot turns or slides in order to push off the pitcher's plate, this is acceptable as long as contact is maintained. It is not considered a step if the pitcher slides his foot across the plate.

D. **Start of Pitch.** The start of the pitch begins when the pitcher takes one hand off the ball or makes any motion that is part of his windup or delivery.

E. **Windup.** The windup may not be two full revolutions. The pitcher's hand may go past the hip twice as long as there are not two complete revolutions. The wrist may not be any farther from the hip than the elbow. The windup may not have a stop or reversal of the forward motion.

F. **Step or Release.** A step (only one) must be taken and it must be **forward**, toward the batter and within the 24-inch length of the pitcher's plate. Dragging or pushing off with the pivot foot from the plate is required of **female adult and female Junior Olympic pitchers. Male adult and male Junior Olympic pitchers** are allowed to have both feet in the air during the forward step. This leap is legal only in male competi-

tion. Pushing off from a spot other than the pitcher's
plate is considered a crow hop and is illegal. The
release of the ball must be simultaneous with the step.
(See Rule 1 for definitions of a crow hop and leaping.)

27. PITCHER'S UNIFORM.
A pitcher should be dressed identically to other players
on the team. A long-sleeved sweatshirt of any color is
acceptable under the jersey. If two players (including the
pitcher) have sweatshirts on, they must be identical in
color and style. No player may wear ragged, frayed or slit
sleeves on an exposed undershirt.

A pitcher may wear a batting glove and/or wristband on
the glove hand and wrist. The batting glove may be white.
A pitcher may wear the pitcher's toe plate on his shoe.

(Fast Pitch Only) Nothing may be on the pitching wrist
or hand, including a band-aid.

(Slow Pitch Only) A pitcher may wear a wristband on his
pitching arm, can have tape on the pitching fingers and
wear any color fielder's glove.

28. PROTESTED GAME UPHELD AND RESCHEDULED.
When a protested game is upheld, the game is to be
rescheduled from the point at which it was protested.
Although the same lineups are to be used when the game
is resumed, there is no penalty for substitutions legally
placed into the lineups at this time. Even if a player was
not at the protested game, he is legal for substitution
purposes when the game is rescheduled as long as he is
on the roster. If a player was ejected in the original game
after the protest was filed, that player may legally play in
the rescheduled game because he was legally in the game

at the time of the protest, unless the ejection also drew suspension for unsportsmanlike conduct.

29. RUN SCORING ON THE THIRD OUT OF AN INNING.

A run will not score if the third out of the inning is a putout at first base (batter-runner) or at another base if a preceding runner is forced because of the batter-runner becoming a runner.

Missed bases could result in a force out. (i.e., If the runner from first base missed second base on a base hit and that was the third out of the inning when properly appealed, any run(s) scored would not count.)

An appeal play on a runner leaving a base too soon on a caught fly ball is considered a time play and not a force. If the appeal results in the third out, any runners preceding the appealed runner would score if they crossed home plate prior to the out.

30. RUNNER HIT BY A FAIR BALL.
A. **While in Contact With the Base.** The runner will never be called out. The ball remains live or dead depending on the closest defensive player. If the closest defensive player is in front of the base the runner is in contact with, the ball is live. However, if the closest defensive player is behind the base, the ball is dead.
B. **While Not in Contact With the Base.** The runner will be called out or ruled safe depending on the interference rule. (Rule 8, Section 8 K & L or Rule 8, Section 9 D-F)

31. SHOES.
Metal cleats are legal in adult male or adult female fast pitch and slow pitch. They are not legal in adult coed

slow pitch play, seniors play, or any level of youth fast pitch or slow pitch. Polyurethane or plastic cleats shaped to look like a metal triangle toe or heel plate are illegal in youth, seniors, and coed play also. If there are nubbins or round plastic cleats in addition to the triangle plate, the shoe is legal. Cleats that screw onto a post are illegal, but cleats that screw into the shoe are legal.

32. SHORTHANDED TEAMS

A team may continue a game with one player less than it uses to begin a game as long as the player vacancy is not created by an ejection. This rule is designed to avoid forfeits whenever possible. In all cases, a team must have a full lineup of players to begin a contest.

In slow pitch, a team must begin with 10 (or if using an EP, with 11), however, they may continue to play with nine (or 10) if a player has to leave the game for any reason other than ejection, and they do not have a substitute on the bench. In the men's senior division where 11 or 12 players can be used, they can play with 11 under the same conditions. The same applies to fast pitch, a team must begin with nine (or if using the DP, with 10), however, they may continue to play with one less.

The following guidelines should be followed in administering this rule:

A. If a team is short one player due to a player being disqualified in Class C or D divisions for excessive home runs, the game is not forfeited. If the team is already playing shorthanded and the disqualification occurs, then the game will be forfeited.

B. If a player leaving the game is a baserunner, the runner is declared out even if the runner reached the base safely.

C. Whenever the absent player is due to bat, an out is

declared. This is the same in coed play, therefore two males or two females cannot follow each other in the batting order without an out.

D. When a team plays shorthanded because a player leaves the game, the player cannot return to the lineup. EXCEPTION: A player being treated under the blood rule can return. (Rule 4, Section 8 C)

E. If there is an eligible substitute at the game, or if an eligible substitute arrives before the game is over, the substitute must enter the game.

F. A team cannot play with two fewer than they started with. The game is forfeited.

NOTE: If the team has only 10 players, one is injured in the third inning, a substitute arrives in the fifth inning and is entered in the game, and another player becomes injured, this is legal as the team can continue to play with nine. If the same team did not have a substitute when the second person was injured, reducing the number of players to eight, the game is forfeited. Playing shorthanded is not a strategic option for a coach. The purpose of this rule is to allow all players on a team to play without fear of injury or illness that previously created a forfeit.

33. STEALING (Slow Pitch).

Base stealing is illegal in slow pitch; however, the runner is not out. Since the ball is dead on balls and strikes, he is returned to the base held at the time of the pitch. Because he cannot steal, he may not be picked off either. A runner may be called out for failure to keep contact with a base to which he is entitled until a legally pitched ball is batted, touches the ground or has reached home plate.

34. SUBSTITUTIONS.

All substitutions must be reported to the plate umpire

who, in turn, will report the changes to the official score-keeper. All substitute names and numbers should be listed on the official lineup card submitted to the plate umpire at the start of the game; however, if a player is not listed on the card and is on the official roster, he can be added after the game has begun.

If a substitution is in the game without reporting, he is considered an **unreported substitute**. If brought to the plate umpire's attention by the offended team after the first legal or illegal pitch and before the team in violation informs the umpire, the umpire will eject him from the game. (Refer to Rule 4, Section 6 B for various situations.)

If a manager removes a substitute from the game and re-enters the same substitute later in the game, this is considered an illegal re-entry. For an illegal re-entry, the player and his manager are ejected. This would not be a forfeit. The only time a game is forfeited for a substitution violation is when a player removed by the umpire (illegal player) is back in the same game.

Violation of any substitution rule is handled as a protest by the offended team.

35. TIE GAMES OR GAMES CALLED WHICH ARE LESS THAN REGULATION.

When these games are rescheduled, the same procedure should be followed as stated in POE #28, PROTESTED GAME UPHELD AND RESCHEDULED.

In determining tie games after five innings (regulation game) have been played, the home team must have had the opportunity to bat and tie the score. If it has scored more runs than the visiting team and the game is called in the bottom of the fifth or sixth inning, the home team shall be the winner. If the visiting team has scored more runs than the home team in the sixth or seventh inning and the home team has not had the opportunity to complete its turn at bat, the game reverts back to the previous inning. If that score was tied, it would be a tie game. If the score was not tied, a winner would be declared if one team was ahead and five full innings had been played.

If a game is called before five full innings have been played (four and one-half if the home team is ahead), the game will be resumed at the point at which it was called.

36. TIE BREAKER RULE.

During each half inning of the inning used to enforce the tie breaker, the offensive team shall begin its turn at bat with the player who is scheduled to bat ninth in that respective half inning being placed at second base. (e.g., If the number five batter is to lead off, the number four batter in the batting order will be placed on second base. A substitute may be inserted for the runner.)

It is the responsibility of the umpire and scorekeeper to notify the teams involved as to what player starts at second base. If the wrong player is placed on the base and it is brought to the umpire's attention, there is no penalty. Correct the error and place the correct person on the base. This should occur whether a pitch has been thrown, or if the runner has advanced a base. If a substitute has been entered without reporting and one pitch has been thrown, the umpire should enforce the illegal substitute penalty when it is brought to his attention.

In scoring, the run scored by a player starting as a runner at second base shall be charged to the defensive team and not the pitcher. Depending on the judgement of the official scorekeeper, a run scored by any other player will be charged to the pitcher's ERA.

Softball
Official Rules

PLAYING RULES
AND
POINTS OF EMPHASIS
INDEX

PLAYING RULES
AND POINTS OF EMPHASIS INDEX

References are by game, rule, section and article.
If a subject is explained in the Points of Emphasis, it is so noted
by a number referring to the section where it can be located.
(i.e., Appeals—POE #1)

Game Key: Specific game not indicated, refer to ALL games.
FP - Fast Pitch
SP - Slow Pitch
MP - Modified Pitch
16" - Sixteen-inch Slow Pitch

Softball
Official Rules

APPENDIX

DIAGRAM 1
SOFTBALL DIAMOND

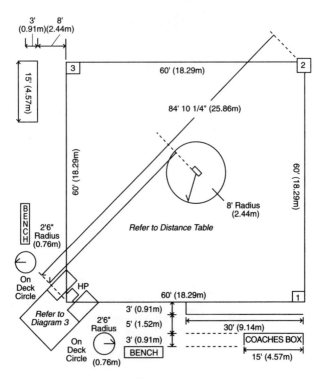

For base distances, pitching distances, and fence distances, see Rule 2, Section 1.

DIAGRAM 2
HOME PLATE TO SECOND BASE

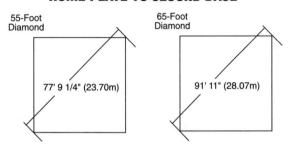

55-Foot Diamond — 77' 9 1/4" (23.70m)

65-Foot Diamond — 91' 11" (28.07m)

DIAGRAM 3
HOME PLATE DETAILS AND CATCHER'S BOX

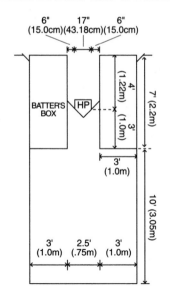

6" (15.0cm) 17" (43.18cm) 6" (15.0cm)

BATTER'S BOX

HP

4' (1.22m)

3' (1.0m)

7' (2.2m)

3' (1.0m)

10' (3.05m)

3' (1.0m) 2.5' (.75m) 3' (1.0m)

DIAGRAM 4
PITCHER'S PLATE

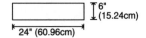

6"
(15.24cm)

24" (60.96cm)

DIAGRAM 5
ON DECK CIRCLE

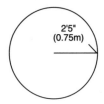

2'5"
(0.75m)

DIAGRAM 6
HOME PLATE

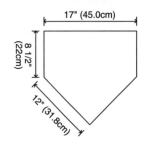

17" (45.0cm)

8 1/2"
(22cm)

12" (31.8cm)

DIAGRAM 7
BASE

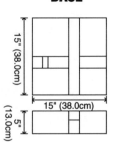

15" (38.0cm)

15" (38.0cm)

5"
(13.0cm)

DIAGRAM 8
INFIELD, OUTFIELD, AND BACKSTOP

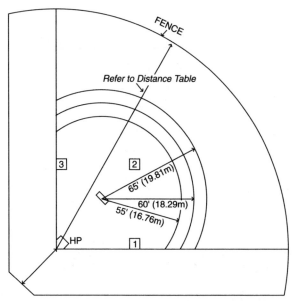

Backstop should be a minimum of 25' (7.62m) or a maximum of 30' (9.14m) from home plate.

Skinned Infields: A 55' (16.76m) and 60' (18.29m) radius may be used with the front center of the 46'(14.02m) pitcher's plate as the center point of the arc. The 60' (18.29m) is recommended for 60' bases. For 65' bases, a 65' (19.81m radius is recommended.

*ASA Playing Rules will be in effect in all college softball
with these modifications.*

NAIA MODIFICATIONS

The Amateur Softball Association (ASA) rules shall be followed by all NAIA affiliate programs for the 1995 season, with the following changes or modifications:

RULE 2, SECTION 3

The pitching distance will be 43 feet.

NCAA MODIFICATIONS

It was determined that the changes or modifications to the ASA rules would be divided into two groups: those modifications used only in championships, and those modifications that institutions must use in the championships as well as in the regular season in order to count when being considered for selection.

CHAMPIONSHIPS ONLY

1. **Enclosed Facility.** The complex must be enclosed so admission can be charged.
2. **Field requirements.** The field must have a skinned infield, an outfield fence, and there must be 25 feet (maximum 30 feet) from home plate to the backstop. For Division 1 and 3, sideline fences are required and recommended for Division 2.
3. **Regional and Final Games Only.** For Division 1, the distance to the outfield fence may not exceed 220 feet. Outfield fences shall be a minimum of 190 feet in left and right fields and 220 feet in center field. All

portable fencing must be secured so as to prevent ball from rolling under the fence.

4. The International Tie Breaker will not be used in championship play.

5. All pitching rules and regulations are to be strictly enforced under Rule 6 of the ASA playing rules.

REGULAR SEASONS AND CHAMPIONSHIPS

1. The pitching distance shall be 43 feet.

2. The lineup becomes official when it is submitted to the umpire.

3. In addition to wearing caps, visors, knee pads, and lycra tights, players on the same team may also wear headbands as defined by the ASA, provided they are alike in make and color (must be a team color), and do not include any visible commercial identification larger than 1½ inches square in size.

4. The pitcher shall not, at any time during the game, be allowed to use any foreign substance on the ball, the pitching hand or fingers, nor shall any other player apply a foreign substance on the ball. Under the supervision and control of the umpire, powdered resin may be used to dry the hands.

   EXCEPTION: the pitcher's hand, wrist, forearm, or elbow may be taped for injury or injury protection, providing such tape is not the color of the ball. The pitcher shall not wear a sweatband, bracelet, or similar type item on the wrist or forearm of the pitching arm.

5. A chest protector must be worn by the catcher.

6. All pitching rules and regulations are to be strictly enforced under rule 6 or the ASA playing rules.

7. The official NCAA ball will be Optic Yellow with red stitches and have a COR of .50 and below.

NJCAA FAST PITCH SOFTBALL RULES

SECTION 5. RULES AND PROCEDURES

a. Current ASA Rules will be used with the following exceptions:

    1. Catchers are required to wear helmets.

    2. The pitching distance shall be 43 feet.

    3. No International tie breaking rule for tournament play.

    4. The eight run rule shall be used in tournament play.

b. The tournament shall be conducted as a double elimination fast pitch tournament.

c. All region/district hosts will use and be furnished the official tournament ball in all post-season play with the exception of regions within a district, which will receive balls only for a district tournament.

d. The official tournament ball is the Dudley WT12YFP.

NJCAA SLOW PITCH SOFTBALL RULES

a. Current ASA rules will be used.

b. ASA official 11-inch softballs (co-efficient of .47) shall be used.

c. The 12-run rule will be in effect after the 5th inning except in the championship game(s).

d. Helmets and masks for catchers are recommended for the National Invitational Softball Tournaments.

e. Steel cleats may not be worn by participating players.

IMPORTANT INFORMATION ABOUT ASA · USA SOFTBALL

The Amateur Softball Association has many important responsibilities as the "national governing body" of amateur softball in the United States including regulating competition to assure fairness and equal opportunity to the thousands of teams, umpires and sponsors who play the sport.

ASA DISTINCTIONS INCLUDE:
THE NATIONAL GOVERNING BODY OF SOFTBALL
MEMBER OF THE UNITED STATES OLYMPIC COMMITTEE
MORE THAN 270,000 TEAMS REGISTERED NATIONALLY
MORE THAN 67,500 JUNIOR OLYMPIC (YOUTH) TEAMS
64 NATIONAL CHAMPIONSHIPS
MORE THAN 58,000 TRAINED AND REGISTERED UMPIRES

The ASA has become one of the nation's largest and fastest growing amateur sports organizations. It now sanctions play in every state through a network of 100 state/metro organizations in 15 regions. The organization annually registers over 270,000 teams combining to form a membership of over 4.5 million.

USA SOFTBALL...REALIZING THE DREAM

The latest and greatest story in softball occurred in 1991 with the addition of women's fast pitch softball to the program of the 1996 Olympic Games in Atlanta.

Working with the United States Olympic Committee (USOC), it is the ASA's responsibility to ensure that our national team has the best possible chance of winning. Under the direction of the ASA, the USA Softball Women's National Team will head into the 1996 Olympic Games as favorite for the gold medal.

JUNIOR OLYMPIC PROGRAM

The ASA has made an investment in the future of softball with its ever growing Junior Olympic program. Each year, more than one million boys and girls across the United States play ASA Junior Olympic softball.

VOLUNTEER IMPROVEMENT PROGRAM

The ASA's Volunteer Improvement Program (VIP) program is designed to help coaches progress through their coaching careers and insure the nation's finest instruction for tomorrow's softball All-Americans.

UMPIRE PROGRAM

Each year, more than 58,000 ASA umpires officiate games organized and promoted by the ASA's associations. Certification as an International Softball Federation (ISF) umpire is the ultimate honor to be achieved by an ASA umpire. Certification on this level allows the umpire to represent the USA as an umpire in ISF sanctioned World Championships, the Pan American Games and the Olympics.

NATIONAL SOFTBALL HALL OF FAME AND MUSEUM

For those players that aspire to greatness in the sport, none can achieve a greater honor than induction into the National Softball Hall of Fame which recognizes the best in the game through special exhibits at the National Softball Hall of Fame in Oklahoma City.

For more information on ASA·USA Softball or for the name of representative in your area, please call (405) 424-5266.

USA SOFTBALL
MAGAZINE

A "MUST READ" FOR ANYONE WHO LOVES SOFTBALL!

Player Profiles • Olympic Softball Updates
Softball Trends • Championship Standings
Milestones & Memories

SIX COLOR ISSUES

**Here's what you've been waiting for,
a magazine totally devoted to your
favorite sport!**

SPECIAL OFFER!

Regularly $16. Now just $12. Please send your check or
money order today to: *USA Softball® Magazine*, 2801
N.E. 50th Street, Oklahoma City, OK 73111-7203 or use
your Visa or MasterCard and order at 1-800-654-8334.